D1468291

163
to
1,20
ℓ

Library of
Cobb Divinity School
No. 1980

: P1 . 01

NEW LIGHT ON THE
LIFE OF JESUS

NEW LIGHT ON THE LIFE OF JESUS

BY

CHARLES AUGUSTUS BRIGGS, D.D., D.Litt.

*Edward Robinson Professor of Biblical Theology
The Union Theological Seminary, New York*

NEW YORK
CHARLES SCRIBNER'S SONS
1904

TROW DIRECTORY
PRINTING AND BOOKBINDING COMPANY
NEW YORK

PREFACE

THIS volume does not propose to give a new life of Jesus Christ our Saviour; but to give a new light upon the life of our Lord which has come to the author in his recent studies. In the term 1861–62 of the Union Theological Seminary, it was my privilege to study with my classmates the Greek Harmony of the Gospels under the greatest of American Biblical scholars, Edward Robinson. An entire year was given to this study at that time. Subsequently in 1867 and 1868 I renewed this study, but from a more historical point of view, at the University of Berlin, under the guidance of one of the greatest theologians of the past century, Isaac Dorner. I then reviewed the entire literature of the Life of Jesus in those troublous times which were dominated by the negative criticism of Strauss, Baur, Renan, Schenkel, and Keim. As a result of these studies I made a revision of Robinson's Harmony for my private

use.   My studies for many years, from 1874–
1891 were concentrated upon the Old Testament, because I was called to use my utmost
endeavors in battling for the rights of the
Higher Criticism and in the work of reconstruct-
ing the Old Testament material in the light of
that Criticism.   In 1891 when I was transferred
from the Hebrew chair to the new chair of
Biblical Theology, it was necessary for me to
renew my New Testament studies and to con-
centrate my attention upon them.   It was in-
evitable that I should apply the same rigorous
methods of Criticism to the New Testament
that I had applied for many years to the Old
Testament.   I had the advantage of coming to
the New Testament afresh from studies in the
Hebrew and Aramaic Scriptures, and so was
prepared to investigate and discern the Sem-
itic originals at the basis of the New Testament.

The Harmony of Robinson was based on the
chronological order of the Gospel of John.   This
order I abandoned many years ago.   But it was
only gradually that my confidence in the chronological order of Mark was weakened.   One of
these pre-suppositions, or both, are at the basis
of the Harmonies of the Gospels and Lives of

Jesus of modern times. So soon as these pre-
suppositions were abandoned, and I felt as free
to study the whole material as Tatian, the earliest harmonist, did, a cloud was lifted from the
Gospels and a number of questions sprang up
which pressed for a solution. The most essential
of these were :

1. When did Jesus begin His Ministry ?
2. Where was Jesus during the absence of the
Twelve? The answer to these two questions
which came to me flooded the Gospels with new
light. I saw that there was a Galilean Ministry
of Jesus prior to the arrest of John the Baptist, and that while five pairs of the Twelve
were absent on a Mission in Galilee, Jesus with
James and John, one pair of the Twelve, was
carrying on His ministry in Jerusalem, and at
intervals with another pair, Thomas and Matthew, in Peræa; and so the order of the ministry
became altogether different from that pre-sup-
posed in the modern Harmonies and Lives of
Jesus.

At first the result was startling, but I was
encouraged by finding that my results were in
many respects in accord with that ancient harmonist, Tatian, and by recalling that the ordinary
arrangement of the Life of Jesus is indeed quite

modern. It was not, however, until I began to
trace the consequences of this new arrangement
of the ministry in all its details, and I saw the
material of the Gospels take its place with so
much ease, so much propriety, and with such
simplicity and beautiful harmony, that I was
convinced that the essential problems of the
Gospels had been solved.

Ten years ago I said: " We would prefer
some chronological scheme. But such a chronological scheme is sufficiently difficult in the
study of the life of the Messiah. It is still more
difficult when we have to put His discourses in
their historical relations. Any attempt to do
this burdens us with numberless questions of
historical criticism where it is impossible at present to attain definite results in some of the
most important passages. Many attempts have
been made to trace a development in the Messianic consciousness of Jesus, and in His doctrine
of the kingdom of God, but none of these has
found favor. It seems impracticable in the
present stage of the criticism of the Gospels to
give an accurate and comprehensive statement of
such a development. It is sufficiently difficult
if the study is limited to the Synoptics. It is at
present impossible if the Gospel of John is in-

cluded in the study." (*Messiah of the Gospels*, pp. 72–73.)

But now I have arranged the Life of Jesus in a simple and orderly chronological scheme. I have also traced the Messianic idea from its origin in a historical situation, in its development in accordance with historical circumstances, even to its climax. I have also traced in a volume soon to be published an orderly development in the entire Ethical Teaching of Jesus.

This new light solves most of the difficult problems of the Gospels, fills up the chasm between the Synoptists and the Gospel of John, and satisfies the most searching inquiries of modern Higher Criticism and Historical Criticism. I have subjected these results to the most careful criticism that I could apply to my own work, again and again. It may be that I have myself been to some extent blinded by the new light. If so I shall be glad to be corrected. The book must go into the fires of criticism, the hotter the better. If the light is a true light it will abide. The question is submitted with confidence to Christian scholars and to the Christian public.

The references to the author's previous works are given without mention of his name. He has avoided discussions of the opinions of other scholars, not because he undervalues them but to make the volume as untechnical as possible and to set forth distinctly the new view he proposes.

Chapters I., III., and IV. were printed as articles in the *Expository Times*, September, October, and November, 1903, and are reprinted with few additions.

CONTENTS

NEW LIGHT ON THE LIFE OF JESUS

I

WHEN DID JESUS BEGIN HIS MINISTRY?

ONE of the most difficult questions connected with the early ministry of Jesus
is : when Jesus began His ministry. The four
Gospels differ in their statements. According
to the Gospel of Mark " *after that John was
delivered up, Jesus came into Galilee, preaching
the gospel of God, and saying, The time is fulfilled, and the kingdom of God is at hand: repent
ye, and believe in the gospel.*" [1] It is a sure result
of the modern criticism of the Gospels, that the
Gospels of Matthew and Luke used Mark as a
source, but with freedom, usually condensing,
but sometimes enlarging and explaining. In
Matthew we find: "*Now when he heard that
John was delivered up, he withdrew into Galilee ;*

---

[1] Mark i. 14, 15.

[*and leaving Nazareth, he came and dwelt in
Capernaum, which is by the sea, in the borders of
Zebulun and Naphtali: that it might be fulfilled
which was spoken by Isaiah. . . .*] From
*that time began Jesus to preach, and to say,
Repent ye; for the kingdom of heaven is at
hand.*"[1] It is evident that all the material in
brackets[2] is an addition to the source. The
other verses give essentially the same as Mark,
but with important modifications, which we
shall consider later on. Luke tells us: "*And
Jesus returned in the power of the Spirit into
Galilee:* [*and a fame went out concerning him
through all the region round about. And he
taught in their synagogues, being glorified of
all.*"][3] It is evident that the bracketed material[4]
is an addition to the source, and that while the
phrase "*in the power of the Spirit*" is unique, the
reference to the agency of the Spirit is charac-
teristically Lukan, and is original with this Gospel. There remains, therefore, as derived from
the Markan source, only "*and Jesus returned into
Galilee*"; the reference to the arrest of John the
Baptist being omitted altogether. Luke is com-

---

[1] Matt. iv. 12–17.
[2] Verses 13–16.
[3] Luke iv. 14, 15.
[4] Verses 14b, 15.

monly recognized to be the best historian in the New Testament, the writer from whom we would expect historical data more than from any other. It is contrary to this characteristic that he should omit such a definite statement as that given in Mark with reference to John the Baptist, if he regarded it as a correct historical statement. We are compelled to the opinion that Luke did not think the ministry of Jesus in Galilee began subsequent to the arrest of John the Baptist. In this he is sustained by the Gospel of John,[1] which gives a ministry of Jesus in Galilee and Judæa prior to the arrest of John, and gives another motive for departing into Galilee a second time. This is the statement: *" When therefore the Lord knew how that the Pharisees had heard that Jesus was making and baptizing more disciples than John, . . . he left Judæa, and departed again into Galilee.*[2]

On the surface of the statements of the Gospels there are grave discrepancies in which Mark and Matthew, on the one side, seem to date the beginning of the Galilean ministry subsequent to the arrest of the Baptist, while Luke and John do not; the latter asserting a ministry in Galilee

---

[1] John 2, 3.

[2] John iv. 1–3.

prior to that event. Those harmonists who regard the Gospel of John as unhistorical, build on the statement of Mark and make the Galilean ministry begin in fact after the arrest of the Baptist, without giving the silence of Luke its due value. Those who accept the historicity of the Gospel of John endeavor to arrange an earlier Galilean ministry, so far as the statements of that Gospel are concerned; but put all the Synoptic material subsequent to the arrest of the Baptist. This does not, however, escape the difficulty, but only makes the discrepancy more glaring. If we build on the statement of Luke, there is no reason why we should not put a considerable amount of the Synoptic material before the arrest of the Baptist. If the statement of Mark is invalid as to the ministry reported by the Gospel of John, it is no less invalid as to the Galilean ministry of Luke's report, and should be no barrier to the consideration of any evidence that may lead to a larger Galilean ministry before the arrest of the Baptist, even to the inclusion of a considerable amount of material given by Mark himself subsequent to his statement. It has been a serious mistake to make this statement of Mark the key to the early ministry of our Lord. It is impossible to make any satisfactory har-

mony of the Gospels on that basis. It is much
safer to build on the statement of Luke.

There are several possible explanations of the
relation of Luke's statement to that of Mark.
The statement of Mark was before Luke in its
present form, and he either (1) rejected it as unhistorical, or (2) interpreted it as not referring
to the real beginning of the Galilean ministry.
(3) Having related the arrest of John,[1] he saw
no reason to refer to it again here. (4) The
statement of Mark in its present form is not that
of the original Mark which Luke used, but the
reference to the Baptist is one of the additions
made to the primitive Gospel. We shall consider these in the inverse order.

It is recognized by all critics that the Greek
canonical Mark has some material which was
not in the original Mark at the basis of the Gospels. How much this material may be, and
what in particular may be regarded as additional,
depends upon careful criticism. Certainly there
is no evidence that Luke had this statement as
to John the Baptist before him, or that the
author of the Gospel of John knew of it. Did
Matthew's Gospel build on the present text of

---

[1] Luke iii. 19.

Mark? This is possible, but by no means certain. It is difficult to see why Matthew should change the statement of the fact in Mark to the *hearing* about it. The structure of the sentence is quite different in Matthew from Mark, although, apart from the addition of *hearing*, both might be regarded as translations of a common Hebrew original. It is altogether probable that "*the gospel of God*" and "*and believe in the gospel*" of Mark are additions to the original Mark. They are not in Matthew. The original Gospel gave only "*preaching and saying, The kingdom of God is at hand: repent ye.*" Resch thinks that the previous clause, "*the time is fulfilled,*" was there also. That is quite possible. In any case, the Greek Mark has at least two clauses of additions to the original Hebrew Gospel, and if so,[1] why not also in the reference to John's arrest? The most that can be said therefore is that it is not certain whether the clause, "*after that John was delivered up,*" was in the original Mark or not.

If it were in the original Mark how could Luke the historian destroy its historical importance by omitting it here and giving the arrest of

---

[1] Mark i. 14b, 15.

John a topical order in the previous chapter?
The question then remains, was it designed to
state the actual beginning of the Galilean ministry, and if so, was it so understood by Luke?
The statement is in the protasis of a temporal
clause, whose apodosis is a general statement as
to the substance of the preaching of Jesus in
Galilee, namely, the proclamation of the advent
of the kingdom of God and the call to repentance, which was also essentially the message of
the Baptist. This is as much as to say that
after the arrest of John the Baptist, Jesus went
into Galilee to preach the same message that the
Baptist had preached. It does not necessarily
imply that Jesus did not teach or work miracles
before the arrest of John, unless we suppose that
this was designed as a comprehensive statement
of His entire work. But that opinion cannot be
sustained. The statement might be interpreted
as a general introductory statement with reference to His ministry in Galilee as a whole, without the necessary implication that all the events
mentioned subsequently, even in Mark, actually
followed the arrest of the Baptist; unless we insist upon strict chronological order for all the
material of this Gospel. But the modern view,
that the order of Mark is the norm for the life of

Jesus, has been so shattered by recent criticism, that it can no longer be regarded as a decisive test in any question. In fact, none of the Gospels can be relied upon for chronological order. They are all dominated by didactic considerations, which make the topical order prevail over the chronological. The ambiguity of the sentence in Mark involving the possibility that it might be interpreted as making the ministry of Jesus in Galilee begin with the arrest of the Baptist, would be a sufficient motive for Luke to omit it.

Matthew's statement is: " *From that time* (defined not only by the arrest of the Baptist and Jesus' withdrawal to Galilee, but also by the leaving Nazareth to dwell in Capernaum) *began Jesus to preach, and to say, Repent ye ; for the kingdom of heaven is at hand.*" This represents that there was a real beginning, not simply with the arrest of the Baptist, but in connection with this removal to Capernaum after the arrest of the Baptist. If we could distinguish between the ministry of preaching the kingdom and an earlier ministry of teaching and miracle-working, then this would be a second stage in the Galilean ministry of Jesus, which would by no means exclude an earlier ministry of a simpler kind.

There are reasons for regarding this distinction as in a measure correct, although it is not clear in fact to any of the evangelists. Prior to the death of the Baptist, Jesus naturally was in his shadow. The Baptist was in the public eye the principal; Jesus appeared rather as his most prominent disciple. It might well be, therefore, that Mark, and even his authority, Peter, conceived of the earlier ministry of Jesus as introductory and relatively unimportant, and that His own real independent ministry began after the death of the Baptist. At all events, there is a dilemma, so far as I can see, for those who regard the statements of John 2–3 as historical. They must either give these statements of Mark some such explanation as those suggested above, or else regard the reference to the arrest of John in this connection as unhistorical. We should not shrink from this latter alternative, if the other could not be sustained.[1]

The story of Luke is intrinsically most probable. The baptism by the Divine Spirit was im-

---

[1] It is noteworthy that Tatian, the earliest harmonist of the Gospels, does not hesitate to ignore this statement of Mark. This fact had escaped my attention until after I had made up my mind on the subject. I was gratified to be sustained by so early and so great an authority.

mediately followed by an ecstatic condition of fasting in the wilderness, at the conclusion of which Jesus endures the great temptation. Returning from the wilderness, He goes under the power of the Spirit to undertake His ministry in Galilee.

The statements of the Gospel of John are entirely harmonious with this. It was natural that on His way to Galilee He should stop at the Jordan side to revisit the one who had baptized Him and given Him the anointing for His ministry.

The recognition of His Messiahship by the Baptist, and the transfer of two of his disciples, Andrew and probably John, to Jesus, and the call of Philip the next day, are altogether in place. With these three disciples He attends a marriage feast at Cana of Galilee on the third day afterward, and then goes down to Capernaum.[1] The naming of Peter[2] and the call of Nathanael[3] were evidently inserted. for topical reasons. They belong to a much later date, as I have shown elsewhere.[4]

---

[1] John i. 29–ii. 12.   [2] John i. 41, 42.
[3] John i. 45–51.

[4] *General Introduction to the Study of Holy Scripture,* pp. 514 *seq.   The Apostolic Commission,* Art. i. in *Studies in Honor of B. L. Gildersleeve.*

We have now to consider the material of the Galilean ministry given by the Synoptists subsequent to the statements considered above. So far as Luke is concerned, there is no reason why all of this should be subsequent to the arrest of the Baptist. We have seen that the statements of Mark and Matthew should not compel us to that opinion. Luke gives first of all in the Galilean ministry Jesus' rejection at Nazareth.[1] But this is only a variation of the story of His rejection given in Mark and Matthew[2] at a much later date. Jesus could not have challenged His townsmen to accept Him as Messiah so early in His ministry. Luke placed this crisis at Nazareth at the beginning of the Galilean ministry for topical reasons. We should not hesitate to place it later, as do Mark and Matthew.

The call of the four fishermen comes first in Mark,[3] and it fits on appropriately to the calls mentioned in John. This is followed by the Sabbath day in Capernaum,[4] and a tour of teaching and miracle-working in Galilee.[5] The Synoptists differ slightly in the order of these events.

---

[1] Luke iv. 16–30.   [2] Mark vi. 1–6a.; Matt. xiii. 54–58.

[3] Mark i. 16–20; Matt. iv. 18–22; Luke v. 1–11.

[4] Mark i. 21–34; Matt. viii. 14–17; Luke iv. 31–41.

[5] Mark i. 35–45; Matt. iv. 23, viii. 1–4; Luke iv. 42–v. 16.

But all give them at this time.   Then comes a
second Sabbath in Capernaum.[1]   This is followed
by the call of Matthew, making the sixth disciple.[2]   All this material seems to belong to the
earlier Galilean ministry, before the arrest of the
Baptist.

The next item in the Synoptists[3] is of some
importance, because it is related in some way to
the narrative of John.[4]   The words of Jesus ad-
dressed to the disciples of the Baptist with reference to fasting are: *" Can the sons of the bride-
chamber fast, while the bridegroom is with them ?
as long as they have the bridegroom with them,
they cannot fast.   But the days will come, when
the bridegroom shall be taken away from them,
and then will they fast in that day."*[5]   These words
seem to imply the word of the Baptist himself :
*" He that hath the bride is the bridegroom : but
the friend of the bridegroom, which standeth and
heareth him, rejoiceth greatly because of the bridegroom's voice : this my joy therefore is fulfilled.
He must increase, but I must decrease."*[6]

Jesus justifies Himself and His disciples over

---

[1] Mark ii. 1–12; Matt. ix. 1–8; Luke v. 17–26.

[2] Mark ii. 13–17; Matt. ix. 9–13; Luke v. 27–32.

[3] Mark ii. 18–22; Matt. ix. 14–17; Luke v. 33–39.

[4] John iii. 22–30.   [5] Mark ii. 19, 20.   [6] John iii. 29, 30.

against the disciples of the Baptist by using the very figure of speech with reference to Himself that the Baptist had used. The discussion between the disciples of Jesus and the disciples of the Baptist as to fasting implies the same essential situation as the discussion as to purifying. Both imply that Jesus was followed by disciples. The disciples present at this time[1] can hardly be explained, unless we suppose that at least several had been previously called. It seems altogether probable, therefore, that Jesus soon after the call of Matthew departed from Galilee to Judæa, and came into connection with the Baptist again,[2] and that in the same region the discussion about fasting took place, as well as that about purification.

The next incident given by Mark[3] and by Luke,[4] although given by Matthew at a later date,[5] is doubtless in its place in Mark. It gives additional evidence of great importance. The disciples on a sabbath day, passing through the fields of ripe grain, pluck some of the ears and rub out the grains and eat them. The ripe grain was still uncut. Leviticus[6] gives the law that

---

[1] John iii. 22.
[3] Mark ii. 23–28.
[5] Matt. xii. 1–8.

[2] John iii. 22–36.
[4] Luke vi. 1–5.
[6] Lev. xxiii. 5–15.

the first-fruits of the barley harvest must be presented as an Omer offering on the morrow after
the first great sabbath, that is, on the second
day of unleavened bread.   Prior to this it was
unlawful to cut the grain or to eat of it.   "*And
ye shall eat neither bread, nor parched corn, nor
fresh ears, until this self-same day.*" [1]   The disciples of Jesus would certainly obey this law,
however far they may have been from the Pharisaic excesses in holding that rubbing grain on
the hands was labor, and so a violation of the
sabbath.   The wheat harvest was two or three
weeks later.   We must therefore conclude that
this incident was subsequent to the Passover,
and not distant from it.   In the text of Luke,
ἐν σαββάτῳ is followed in most early codices [2]
by δευτεροπρώτῳ, and this is accepted by Tisch-
endorf and most critical authorities, although rejected by Westcott and Hort, Weiss,[3] and many
others.   It is a difficult reading, whose omis-
sion is easier to explain than its insertion.
Whether it was original or a later explanatory
addition, it is still important because it defines
that sabbath.   It seems to be the sabbath after

---

[1] Lev. xxiii. 14.   [2] A C D E H K, etc.
[3] These follow too closely B א.

the Omer offering, and therefore Jesus and His disciples were on their way from Jerusalem to Galilee, having just left Jerusalem immediately after the conclusion of Passover. If this be so, then all the events thus far considered, except the last, were prior to the first Passover which Jesus spent with His disciples in Jerusalem. This second return to Galilee would then correspond with that mentioned in John [1] the motive of which was the opposition of the Pharisees of Judæa, due to the wonderful success of Jesus in winning disciples even beyond that of the Baptist. Jesus, for prudential reasons, would avoid a premature conflict with the Pharisees of Jerusalem. There is no sufficient reason to doubt this statement, although it is prefixed to the story of the journey through Samaria, which must be assigned to a much later time in the life of Jesus. [2]

The Gospel of John does not mention the arrest of the Baptist at this stage, and it is probable that it had not yet happened when Jesus departed for Galilee, but that it occurred so soon afterward that it might be assigned by Matthew and Mark as a motive for the beginning of the

[1] John iv. 1–3.   [2] See p. 45.

preaching of the repentance and the near advent of the kingdom of God.

If now we look back over the incidents thus far considered as prior to this, the first Passover of Jesus' ministry, we may conclude that the first meeting of Jesus with the Baptist was due to His journey from Galilee to Jerusalem to keep the Feast of Tabernacles, and that it was on His return from this feast that He went alone to the Baptist to be baptized by him in the Jordan. The first stage of the ministry of Jesus, therefore, was between Tabernacles and Passover, and this first Passover spent by Jesus and His disciples in Jerusalem marks essentially the boundary between the preparatory work of the Baptist and the ministry of Jesus. The work of Jesus up to this time was a preparatory work under the shadow of the Baptist, and therefore not considered by Mark and his authority, St. Peter, as the real beginning of the ministry of Jesus.

II

JESUS AND JOHN THE BAPTIST

ACCORDING to Luke, Jesus and John the Baptist were near relations through their mothers, Mary and Elizabeth. Although Elizabeth brought up her son in a city in the hill country of Judah, and Jesus was brought up in the distant Nazareth of Galilee, it is altogether probable that other visits were made by Mary to Elizabeth than that reported in Luke; and that at such visits Jesus and John became acquainted as boys. The statement of Luke,[1] that the residence of Elizabeth was in a city of Judah in the hill country, is too indefinite to be accurate. The conjecture of Reland supported by Robinson, that Judah stands for Juttah, a city of the priests south of Hebron,[2] is probably correct. Moreover, Zacharias must have attended the feasts at Jerusalem with his family, and twice in the year he served there in his course as priest in the temple. The visits of Jesus with His par-

---

[1] Luke i. 39.   [2] Josh. xv. 55, xxi. 16.

ents to the feasts gave frequent opportunity for
renewing the acquaintance of Jesus and John
during the eighteen years subsequent to Jesus'
first visit to Jerusalem prior to the beginning of
His ministry.   It is true that John the Baptist
is reported as saying : " *I knew him not ;* " [1]
but the context indicates that this knowledge
was not that of personal acquaintance, but of
recognition of His special calling as Messiah.

Jesus and the Baptist first came into contact
in a public way when Jesus went to him for
baptism.   At this time John, guided by the theophany which he received, recognizes Jesus as
the One greater than himself whom he had
heralded.[2]

Jesus immediately after His Baptism goes
for forty days, in the ecstatic state, into the wilderness, and undergoes His temptation; [3] after
which He visits the Baptist on His way to Galilee and is recognized by him as his Master.   Two
of the Baptist's disciples join Jesus on the following day, and on the third day Jesus returns
to Galilee.[4]

The next meeting of John and Jesus was at

---

[1] John i. 31.

[2] John i. 32–34.

[3] Mark i. 12, 13.

[4] John i. 29–43.

Ænon, near Salim, in the valley of the Jordan.
Jesus in the meantime had gathered about Him
a band of disciples. Jesus and these disciples
teach, make disciples, and baptize alongside of
John and his disciples. The disciples of the
Baptist were disturbed by this apparent rivalry
all the more that Jesus' success was greater than
that of their master.[1] Accordingly disputes
arose respecting purifications[2] and fasting.[3] But
the Baptist distinctly recognized and stated to
his disciples that Jesus must increase while he
himself decreased.[4]

The motive for the departure of Jesus to
Galilee, the second time, as given in John,[5] was
the opposition of the Pharisees to Him because
of His greater success in winning disciples than
John. This naturally implies that Jesus left for
Galilee while John was still working. The
statement of Mark,[6] upon which Matthew[7] is
based, that He withdrew into Galilee after the
arrest of John, is, as we have seen,[8] either incorrect, or was not meant to exclude an introductory Galilean ministry. At all events the

---

[1] John iii. 22–23, 26, iv. 1–2. [2] John iii. 25.
[3] Mark ii. 18–22. [4] John iii. 25–30.
[5] John iv. 1. [6] Mark i. 14.
[7] Matt. iv. 12. [8] See pp. 1 *seq.*

arrest of the Baptist could not have been long after this second departure of Jesus into Galilee and probably it was soon afterward.

The arrest of the Baptist is stated in Mark[1] and Matthew[2] incidentally in connection with their account of the opening of the Galilean ministry. But the Gospels give a fuller account at a much later date, incidentally again, as preparatory to the narrative of the martyrdom of the Baptist.[3] Luke, however, mentions the imprisonment as supplementary to an account of his work.[4] The imprisonment is also mentioned incidentally in Matthew,[5] in connection with the message of the Baptist to Jesus.

There are three important events which are in chronological succession in the closing career of the Baptist: (1) His imprisonment, (2) His message to Jesus, (3) His death. These give us a frame on which we may construct a large part of the Galilean ministry of Jesus.

1. The arrest and imprisonment of the Baptist were due to his prophetic denunciation of Herod for his illegal marriage with Herodias his brother's wife. It is improbable that this could

---

[1] Mark i. 14.   [2] Matt. iv. 12.
[3] Mark vi. 17, 18 ; Matt. xiv. 3–5.   [4] Luke iii. 19, 20.
[5] Matt. xi. 2.

have occurred while Jesus was working with him; otherwise Jesus also would have been under suspicion by Herod and his satellites. It is probable, therefore, that it did not occur until after Jesus had departed into Galilee. But it was probably soon after Jesus arrived in Galilee.

2. The Baptist while in prison sends a message to Jesus through two of his disciples. This message is not given in Mark but in Matthew [1] and Luke.[2] The message was: *"Art Thou he that cometh, or look we for another?"* This does not imply any doubt in the Baptist's mind as to the fact that Jesus was the One he had already proclaimed him to be, as the One greater than himself whose advent it was his privilege to herald. But it implied a doubt whether Jesus in all respects fulfilled the ideal of his prediction. This was due to the complexity of the Messianic ideals of the Old Testament,[3] and also to the fact that the Baptist had heralded the advent of God in a day of judgment. He could not see his way through the mazes of prophetic ideals. Jesus in His reply tells these disciples of the Baptist to report what they have seen and heard.

---

[1] Matt. xi. 2–19.　　　　[2] Luke vii. 18–35.
[3] *The Incarnation of the Lord*, pp. 172 *seq.*

"The blind receive their sight;
The lame walk;
The lepers are cleansed;
The deaf hear;
The dead are raised up;
The poor have good tidings preached to them;
Blessed is he, whosoever shall find none occasion of stumbling
in me."

This logion is practically identical in both reports and probably comes from the Logia of Matthew. It implies therefore a considerable amount of miracle-working and preaching by Jesus. Indeed it was the report of this, that came to the Baptist either by rumor or from the testimony of his disciples, or from both, which was the occasion of the message. We may safely put the following incidents in the second Galilean ministry prior to the message of the Baptist:

(1.) The healing of the man with the withered hand on a sabbath in the synagogue which immediately follows, in the three Synoptists,[1] the story of the plucking of the ears of grain on the sabbath. Matthew puts both of these incidents later, after the sending forth of the Twelve. But Matthew's order is evidently not historical.

---

[1] Mark iii. 1–6 ; Matt. xii. 9–14 ; Luke vi. 6–11.

The order of the other Synoptists is also topical.
The intense hostility of the Pharisees in connection with this healing is too early in the
development of the conflict of Jesus with them.
This event belongs at the close of this visit to
Galilee, just before going to the feast of Pentecost.   For topical reasons it is given out of
place even in Mark.

(2.) The preaching by the seashore [1] comes
next; then,

(3.) The appointment of the Twelve. [2]

(4.) The Sermon on the Mount is really, according to Luke, the discourse of Consecration
of the Twelve. [3] This is enlarged in Matthew
v.–vii., by the addition of a great amount of material selected from logia given on many different occasions, according to Luke.

(5.) The healing of the Centurion's servant in
Capernaum soon follows. [4]   This is doubtless the
same as the similar story of John. [5] It tells us
that Jesus was at Cana when the nobleman
sent to Him to come to Capernaum, which
implies a work in Cana after the Sermon on the
Mount, on the way to Capernaum.

---

[1] Mark iii. 7–12.   [2] Mark iii. 13–19a ; Luke vi. 12–19.
[3] Luke vi. 20–49.   [4] Luke vii. 1–10 ; Matt. viii. 5–13.
[5] John iv. 46–54.

(6.) Luke reports the raising of the widow's son at Nain,[1] prior to the message.

The narratives also imply an extended tour, in which Jesus was followed by multitudes, and during which He wrought many miracles.

Are these incidents sufficient to account for the words of His message to the Baptist? A leper was healed on His first tour.[2] A dead boy was raised in the second tour.[3] But thus far there has been no report of healing the blind, lame, or deaf. Are we justified in including these under the generic terms for healings given in the previous narrative?—or, must we put this message of the Baptist later, after such miracles are reported?—or, if we cannot take either of these alternatives, are we to suppose this logion was not exactly what Jesus said, but a summing up of His miracle-working uttered later and attached by the evangelist here for topical reasons? Luke tells us: "*In that hour he cured many of diseases and plagues and evil spirits; and on many that were blind he bestowed sight.*"[4] But this is not in Matthew and was not derived from the Logia, and may be regarded as an

---

[1] Luke vii. 11–17.   [2] Mark i. 40–45.
[3] Luke vii. 11–17.   [4] Luke vii. 21.

explanatory addition of Luke. In case the
logion was a topical addition to the narrative,
the answer of Jesus to the Baptist would be
simply His words to the two disciples : " *Go
your way, and tell John what things ye have
seen and heard.*" [1] This on the whole, seems
most probable under all the circumstances of
the case. If the view taken in another chapter
be correct [2] that all this took place between
Passover and Pentecost, and that John the Baptist's arrest took place soon after Passover, then
the message must have been sent between thirty
and forty days after the arrest of John.

3. The final catastrophe of the beheading of
the Baptist is reported in the three Synoptists. [3]
This is given incidentally, some time after its occurrence, in connection with Herod's alarm lest
Jesus might be John the Baptist risen from the
dead. The story is given by the three Synoptists
immediately before the Feeding of the multitude.
Mark and Luke let it immediately follow the
Commission of the Twelve. But Matthew inserts a considerable amount of the ministry of
Jesus between the Commission and this story, all

---

[1] Luke vii. 22 ; Matt. xi. 4.   [2] See pp. 15, 52.
[3] Mark vi. 14–29 ; Matt. xiv. 1–12 ; cf. Luke ix. 7–9.

of which is out of place.   There is a great gap here in the narrative of Mark, during the absence of the Twelve, which we shall consider later on.   But at this point we must ask, what, then, was the place of the death of the Baptist in relation to the ministry of Jesus?   It is probable that there was a real connection between the Commission of the Twelve and the death of the Baptist.   The putting of the Baptist to death at the solicitation of Herodias, which Herod commanded with great reluctance, with many scruples, and much anxiety, doubtless made him very sensitive to public opinions and superstitions.   When the miracle-working and preaching of Jesus was reported to him soon afterward, he saw that Jesus was carrying on the work of the Baptist with greater vigor and success, and he feared that John the Baptist had risen from the dead in the person of Jesus.

This put the work of Jesus and Jesus Himself in great peril from Herod and his court. This, therefore, was a reason why Jesus should give over His mission in Galilee to the Twelve, and retire Himself to another and safer field of labor.   If this be so, it is probable that the death of John occurred shortly before the Commission of the Twelve.   We may, therefore, put the most of the remaining Galilean ministry of Jesus prior to the death of the Baptist.

John v. reports a journey of Jesus to Jerusalem at a feast. If this was Pentecost, as we shall show later on,[1] it came a few days after the message of the Baptist to Jesus. In His discourse at this feast Jesus said to the Pharisees— " *Ye have sent unto John, and he hath borne witness unto the truth. . . . He was the lamp that burneth and shineth ; and ye were willing to rejoice for a season in his light.*"[2] Does this imply that the Baptist was still alive or that he was already dead? These words do not suggest the death of the Baptist. It seems probable that if the Baptist had already suffered death, it would have appeared in a reference to him at this time. It is most natural to interpret these words as referring to the testimony of one still living, but whose career had diminished in importance.

John[3] states that after the Feast of Dedication Jesus went into Peræa "*into the place where John was at the first baptizing; and there he abode. And many came unto him; and they said, John indeed did no sign, but all things what-*

---

[1] See p. 52.   [2] John v. 33–35.   [3] John x. 40–41.

soever John spake of this man were true." [1] This
speaks of John as if he were no longer living.
The death of John occurred, therefore, in all
probability between Pentecost and Dedication.
If the view taken in another chapter is correct,[2]
it occurred between Pentecost and Tabernacles.
If, as we suppose, John the Baptist was arrested
soon after Passover, he was put to death on the
subsequent birthday of Herod, a little before
Tabernacles of the same year. It is not likely
that his enemies would allow him to live any
longer than they could help.

Soon after the message of the Baptist Jesus
goes to the Feast of Pentecost, and then returns
for His third mission to Galilee. The earlier incidents are mentioned by Luke alone, namely:

(1) His anointing by a penitent woman in the
house of Simon.[3]

(2) He made a tour through Galilee accompanied by several women as well as His other
disciples.[4]

(3) The three Synoptists report the anxiety
of His family respecting Him, in connection with
which He proclaims the true kinship of the

---

[1] John x. 22.   [2] See p. 43.
[3] Luke vii. 36–50.   [4] Luke viii. 1–3.

family of God.[1]   Mark inserts here,[2] sustained
by Matthew,[3] material given by Luke[4] at a later
and better date.   Probably this material was inserted for topical reasons, and may be an addition to the original Mark.   It is chiefly composed of logia.

(4) Next come the parables of the Kingdom
spoken at the seaside,[5] to which Matthew adds a
number of other parables of the Kingdom spoken
at other times.[6]

(5) Jesus then crosses the sea into the country
of the Gadarenes ; on the way he stills the tempest, and, arriving on the other side, heals a
demoniac.[7]

(6) Returning to the Galilean side of the sea,
Jesus raises Jairus' daughter from the dead, and
cures a woman from an issue of blood.[8]

(7) He then makes a final tour in Galilee,[9]
which may correspond with the one mentioned
in Luke,[10] the latter beginning the narrative with

---

[1] Mark iii. 19b–21, 31–35 ; Matt. xii. 46–50 ; Luke viii. 8–19.

[2] Mark iii. 22–30.   [3] Matt. xii. 22–45.   [4] Luke xi. 14–36.

[5] Mark iv. 1–34 ; Luke viii. 4–18.   [6] Matt. xiii. 1–53.

[7] Mark iv. 35–41, v. 1–20 ;   Luke viii. 22–39 ; Matt. viii.
22–34.

[8] Mark v. 21–43 ; Matt. ix. 18–26 ; Luke viii. 40–56.

[9] Mark vi. 6 ; Matt. ix. 35.   [10] Luke viii. 1–3.

the general statement, the former concluding
with the general statement.

Jesus now hears of the death of the Baptist
and the suspicion of Herod relating to himself,
and He commissions the Twelve to go in pairs
and carry on his Mission in Galilee,[1] to which
Matthew[2] adds many logia given by Luke in
connection with the commission of the Seventy,
and others belonging to the final Apostolic Commission.[3]

---

[1] Mark vi. 7–13 ; Luke ix. 1–6.   [2] Matt. x. 1, 5–xi. 1.

[3] See *The Apostolic Commission*, Art. i. in *Studies in Honor of
B. L. Gildersleeve.*

III

THE TWELVE AND THE SEVENTY

THE Gospels of Mark and Matthew give the sending forth of the Twelve, the Gospel of Luke the sending forth of both the Twelve and the Seventy. The Gospel of John says nothing about either event. It does not mention the Seventy at all. It mentions the Twelve only twice, and even these passages may be redactional. But, on the other hand, this Gospel gives a group of seven disciples, and mentions several names not known to the Synoptists. These differences raise several difficult questions.

The story of Mark[1] is simple. The sending forth of the Twelve in pairs to preach repentance and work miracles is given without explicit motive. The story of the death of John the Baptist is inserted.[2] Then the return of the Twelve is given in connection with the Feeding of the multitudes.[3]

---

[1] Mark vi. 7–13.   [2] Mark vi. 14–29.   [3] Mark vi. 30–46.

The story of Luke[1] is evidently based on
Mark, and gives nothing additional of any importance. But Luke also gives an account of
the sending forth of the Seventy[2] and their
return[3] in connection with a large amount of
material usually supposed to belong to the
Peræan ministry, unknown for the most part to
Matthew and Mark, and evidently derived from
a source unknown to these Evangelists.

A large amount of the material, in the form
of logia, spoken by Jesus in connection with the
sending forth and the return of the Seventy, is
given by Matthew in connection with the mission
and return of the Twelve.[4] Between these is
inserted the sending of the disciples of the
Baptist to Jesus,[5] given by Luke elsewhere. In
fact, as I have shown, Matthew heaps up in this
section a number of logia connected with the
ministry of the disciples, not only those uttered
by Jesus according to Luke on these two different occasions, but also some belonging to the
final commission of the Twelve before His departure from the world to the Father.[6] Many

---

[1] Luke ix. 1–6.   [2] Luke x. 1–16.   [3] Luke x. 17–24.
[4] Matt. x. 1–xi. 1, and xi. 20–27.   [5] Matt. xi. 2–19.
[6] *The Apostolic Commission*, Art. i. in *Studies in Honor of B.
L. Gildersleeve*.

of the logia scattered through those chapters of Luke which are peculiar to him, are found in Matthew attached to his version of the Sermon on the Mount, the Woes of the Pharisees, and the Eschatological Discourse, all derived from the Logia of Matthew by our Gospels of Matthew and Luke, notwithstanding this difference in the grouping of the material.

There is no sufficient reason why we should doubt the mission of this second group of disciples by Jesus. It is altogether probable that the Twelve were commissioned for a Galilean ministry, the Seventy for a Peræan and Judæan ministry. It is a common opinion that Jesus was accompanied by the Twelve throughout His ministry, and that their absence from Him was quite brief. This opinion is due doubtless to the fact that the return from their mission is given in the narrative so close to the sending forth. But this, as in the case of the Seventy also, was due to topical reasons and by no means implies the close proximity in time of the sending and the return. This mission, if it amounted to anything, must have continued several weeks at least.

There are in the Gospels of Matthew and Mark many instances of calls to a special following of Jesus connected with the abandonment of all things else, some accepted, others rejected— calls which imply a larger circle of special disciples than the Twelve, and which, therefore, incidentally sustain another and a larger group of ministers, such as the Seventy of Luke. Only thus can we get a basis in the life of Jesus for the two groups of the apostolic history, the Twelve and the larger group of prophets such as Barnabas, Ananias, Joseph, and Matthias, the latter of whom was assigned the place of Judas in the group of the Twelve. The term *apostle* was not used by Jesus, but was first given at Antioch in connection with the mission of Barnabas and Paul, and was a comprehensive term which was used indifferently for both of these groups.

A careful study of the Gospels shows us that there was indeed a natural and simple development in the calling, training, and sending forth of the ministry by Jesus during His lifetime. The Synoptic narrative tells of the call of the four fishermen and of Matthew. The narrative of John tells us of the call of Andrew and Simon, Philip and Nathanael, and a fifth, probably John. Nathanael is usually regarded as another name for Bartholomew of the Synoptists ; but this is by no means certain. How and when the others named among the Twelve were called by Jesus we are not told. But it was not long before a group of Twelve was selected with Peter at the head.[1]

The Sermon on the Mount, so called, according to the version of Luke which is nearest to the original, was a discourse of consecration. Matthew has attached to it a large amount of material gathered from the Logia of Matthew, given by the other Synoptists on many other different occasions.

After continuing with Jesus as a group of Twelve for some considerable time, they were sent forth in pairs to conduct missions throughout Galilee. At this time Jesus gave them a solemn charge. This mission continued until shortly before the last journey of Jesus to Jerusalem.

It is probable that one of these pairs always remained with Jesus ; at one time John and James, at another Andrew and Peter, at another Matthew and Thomas. But the Twelve, as a whole, were absent on their mission from this time forth until they rejoined Jesus just prior to

---

[1] Mark iii. 13-19 ; Matt. x. 2-4 ; Luke vi. 12-19.

the Feeding of the multitudes, which was only a short time before the Passion of Jesus, and not in the midst of His ministry, as is commonly supposed.

In the meanwhile Jesus was attaching other disciples to Himself besides the Twelve, by special calls, and preparing them for a special ministry. Before setting forth upon His Peræan ministry, He organizes Seventy of these in a group and sends them forth in pairs to prepare the way before Him in Peræa and in Judæa. These also return to Him, probably on His last passage along the border of Peræa on His way to Jerusalem.

The mission of the Seventy is not reported in Mark because that Gospel depends upon the preaching of Peter, and Peter seems to have limited his testimony to that which he himself had seen and heard. He was not present during the Peræan and Judæan ministry of Luke and John, and therefore makes no report of it, or of the work of the Seventy with which he had nothing to do.

The Gospel of Matthew is based on Mark and the Logia of Matthew, which latter [1] was simply

---

[1] See my articles, *Expository Times*, June, July, August, November, 1897.

a collection of the wisdom of Jesus with occasional introductory incidents, but without historical narrative. These the author of our Gospel of Matthew arranged as best he could in groups on the basis of Mark's narrative. He had no knowledge of the special sources used by Luke and John, or of the historical material given in those sources.

If the order in the development of the ministry given above is correct, we have an important help for the arrangement of the material relating to the life of Jesus.

1. The calling of disciples to follow Jesus in a life involving an abandonment of all else.

2. The selection of Twelve of these into a special group, and their solemn setting apart.

3. The mission of these Twelve to Galilee.

4. The selection of a larger group of Seventy, and their consecration.

5. The mission of the Seventy to Peræa and Judæa.

6. The return of the Twelve near Bethsaida in order to accompany Jesus to His last Passover.

7. The return of the Seventy on His last journey along the border of Peræa to Jerusalem.

8. The final commission of the apostolic ministry.

If now we take this as a framework for the material given in the Gospels, it is evident that the usual arrangement of the harmonists is incorrect.

The material Mark vi. 30–ix. = Matt. xiv. 13–xviii. = Luke ix. 10–50 does not precede Luke x.–xviii. 14, but follows it. Luke xviii. 15–34 coincides with Mark x. 13–34. The material inserted here in Luke between ix. 50 and xviii. 15 is material, apart from the logia, derived from another source unknown to Mark and Matthew. Luke does not mingle the material derived from this source with the material derived from Mark, but follows Mark essentially as far as ix. 50, only changing the order occasionally for topical reasons, and then gives his new material entirely by itself. This new material, apart from the logia, belongs for the most part to the Peræan ministry, while Peter was absent from Jesus in Galilee. There is no sound reason which compels us to place this ministry subsequent to the entire Galilean ministry, as the modern harmonists do.

The situation is similar with the material given in John vii. 1–xi. 54. This is based on a source unknown to the Synoptists. There is no sound reason why it should be placed between Mark ix. 50 and Mark x. 2. The single intervening

verse x. 1 may or may not correspond with Luke
ix. 51. The passages are not so similar that a
coincidence is evident. In the former Jesus
goes into the borders of Jordan and Peræa. In
the latter he goes steadfastly toward Jerusalem
through Samaria, which is very different. The
latter probably corresponds with the journey to
the Feast of Tabernacles,[1] to which He went up
secretly through Samaria, the unusual route, to
avoid the publicity of the usual route by the
valley of the Jordan. The former probably was
much later, His last journey on which He cast
all secrecy and prudence aside, and therefore went
to Jerusalem by the usual route with all His
disciples by way of the Jordan, Jericho, and
Bethany.

This arrangement of the material gives a better development to the narrative, explains the
silence of Mark as to the Peræan and Jerusalem
ministry by the absence of Peter, whose preaching was the basis of Mark, and puts a new light
upon many obscure problems.

---

[1] John vii. 1–13.

IV

WHERE WAS JESUS DURING THE ABSENCE OF THE TWELVE?[1]

THE sending forth of the Twelve was for a mission in Galilee.[2] They went in pairs, therefore, in six different circuits. This mission must have taken some considerable time; for it contemplates the going from one city to another and from house to house, and the sojourning for a time in houses and cities, because directions are given respecting just these things. All this could not have been accomplished in a few days. A comprehensive mission seems to have been contemplated so as to reach entire Galilee.

The return is given in close connection with the sending.[3] These Evangelists insert accounts

---

[1] I have asked several eminent New Testament scholars this question, but not one of them had thought of it before, or could give me an answer. So far as I am aware, the harmonists and authors of Lives of Jesus have not considered it.

[2] Mark vi. 7–13; Matt. ix. 36–xi. 1; Luke ix. 1–6.

[3] Mark vi. 30; Luke ix. 10.

of the death of John the Baptist,[1] motived by
the fact that Herod heard of the great work of
Jesus, and was so disturbed by it that he supposed that John the Baptist had risen from
the dead in Jesus. This is given by Matthew[2]
immediately before the Feeding of the multitude, without any mention of the return of
the Twelve. That Gospel inserts a considerable
amount of material here.

(1) An account of the message of the Baptist
to Jesus,[3] which is given by Luke at an earlier
and more probable date.[4]

(2) A number of logia follow,[5] the most of
which are given by Luke more appropriately in
connection with the return of the Seventy.[6]

(3) Matthew also gives, before the Feeding of
the multitudes, various incidents reported by
Mark and Luke at other dates.[7]

---

[1] Mark vi. 14–29 = Luke ix. 7–9   [2] Matt. xiv. 1–12.
[3] Matt. xi. 2–19.   [4] Luke vii. 18–35.
[5] Matt. xi. 20–30.   [6] Luke x. 13–24.
[7] (a) Matt. xii. 1–21 = Mark ii. 23–iii. 12 = Luke vi. 1–11 ;
(b) Matt. xii. 22–50 = Mark iii. 19b–35—incidents given by
Luke at two different times, the former (xi. 14–36) at a later
date, the latter (viii. 19–21) at an earlier date ; (c) Matt. xiii.
1–53, the parables by the sea = Mark iv. 1–34 = Luke viii.
4–18 ; and (d) Matt. xiii. 54–58, the rejection at Nazareth =
Mark vi. 1–6 = Luke iv. 16–30.

Mark and Luke make no statement whatever as to what Jesus did in the absence of the Twelve.   But Matthew tells us :[1] " *And it came to pass, when Jesus had made an end of commanding his twelve disciples, he departed thence to teach and preach in their cities.*" This is a general statement, which this Gospel adds to the Markan source, and is indeed most probable in itself.   But it does not tell us where Jesus carried on His ministry.   It is not probable that He reserved a seventh circuit in Galilee to Himself, or that He went with one pair on one of these circuits.   It is much more probable that having divided up Galilee among the Twelve, He Himself, either alone or, more likely, with one of these pairs, went elsewhere to carry on His ministry.   The insertion of so many incidents by Matthew prior to the Feeding of the multitudes, in connection with which Mark, followed by Luke, gives the return of the Twelve— although Matthew does not mention the return at all—yet implies that the author of this Gospel supposed there was a considerable ministry of Jesus during that interval.   Some of these incidents given by Matthew in this interval really

---

[1] Matt. xi. 1.

belong there. But Mark's order in most cases
is to be preferred; in others, that of Luke.
We must recognize however the effort of the
author of Matthew to fill up this gap.

If it is reasonable to suppose that Jesus, during the absence of the Twelve would carry on
His ministry elsewhere than in Galilee, then we
have a gap of time in which we may place the
Jerusalem ministry of the Gospel of John and
the Peræan ministry of the Gospel of Luke,
both absent from the Gospel of Mark because
Peter was on a mission in Galilee all this time.
And, indeed, this ministry in Jerusalem and
Peræa fits into this space with the utmost ex-
actness and nicety. It is evident from Mark
and Luke that the anxiety of Herod was a real
peril for the continuance of Jesus' work, and was
a sufficient motive for giving over His Galilean
ministry to the Twelve, while He Himself re-
tired elsewhere.

Luke,[1] at the beginning of the material derived
by this Evangelist from another source than
Mark, tells us that Jesus set His face to go to
Jerusalem, and that He went by way of Samaria.
This unusual route to Jerusalem, instead of the

---

[1] Luke ix. 51–56.

usual route by the valley of the Jordan, was doubtless because of the peril from Herod and the need of a secret journey. The brother pair, James and John, accompanied Him on this journey to Jerusalem, as is evident from the first incident in Samaria, where their names are mentioned and no others. There is no evidence of the presence of any others of the Twelve.

This journey may be put in parallelism with the journey described in John.[1] Jesus does not go up to the Feast of Tabernacles with His brethren in a public way, but in secret; and He does not appear in public until the midst of the feast.[2] During this feast the visit to Martha and Mary in Bethany[3] doubtless occurred. It is probable that the Seventy were sent forth from Jerusalem on their mission to Peræa and Judæa. From Jerusalem Jesus follows in the footsteps of the Seventy in a ministry in Peræa,[4] which concludes with a journey to Jerusalem.[5] This journey seems to correspond with that reported in John[6] at the Feast of Dedication, from which He returns to Peræa.[7]

The ministry in Peræa included the incidents

---

[1] John vii. 2–14.   [2] John vii. 10–14.   [3] Luke x. 38–42.

[4] Luke x. 25–37, xi.–xiii. 21.   [5] Luke xiii. 22.

[6] John x. 22–39.   [7] John x. 40.

and teaching mentioned in Luke,[1] for the most part at least, although the exact connection of the logia is by no means certain. From this ministry Jesus is suddenly recalled to Jerusalem by the death of Lazarus.[2] The raising of Lazarus from the dead excited so great attention that Jesus was in great danger from the authorities, and He retires to Ephraim on the borders of Samaria.[3]

It is probable that the journey northward to Galilee through Samaria[4] occurred at this time. He was in peril, both from the authorities of Jerusalem and also from Herod, and the safest journey was just this one. He was on the borders of Samaria at Ephraim, and the journey through Samaria was the easiest from this place. The statement " *Say not ye, There are yet four months, and then cometh the harvest ?* "[5] exactly suits this time. Moreover, the explicit statement of His Messiahship suits this period of His ministry, and could hardly have come much earlier.

The order of the material of John is certainly not chronological but topical, as Tatian recognized.[6] At this time John and James alone of

---

[1] Luke xiv.–xvii. 10.   [2] John xi.   [3] John xi. 54.
[4] John iv. 3–43.   [5] John iv. 35.
[6] He puts the journey through Samaria after Mark vii. 24–37.

the Twelve were with Jesus, and therefore
John's Gospel tells us of these things and
Peter's Gospel does not mention them. Indeed,
these brothers had been with him in Samaria.
They would be especially valuable to Jesus in
Jerusalem because of their important acquaint-
anceship there.[1]   They, if any of the Twelve,
would remain with him during his ministry there,
and return with him through Samaria to Galilee.

Arriving in Galilee, Jesus comes at once into
peril from Herod, and therefore He avoids renewing His ministry in Galilee and hurries
northward to Tyre and Sidon.[2]   It is probable
that the preaching in Nazareth and His rejection
there occurred on His way.   The Synoptists are
in disagreement as to the time.[3]   It is more appropriate here because of the explicit statement
of Jesus' Messiahship with the implication of
His impending sufferings and the hostile temper
of the Nazarenes.[4]

Here Mark resumes his narrative, and it is

---

[1] John xviii. 15–16.   [2] Mark vii. 24–30.

[3] Mark vi. 1–6; Matt. xiii. 54–58; Luke iv. 16–30.

[4] The logion, John iv. 44, certainly was uttered at Nazareth,
and suggests that the discourse at Nazareth immediately followed the journey through Samaria.   As I shall show later,
there has been a displacement of the original John here.
See p. 151.

probable that Peter and Andrew join Jesus at Nazareth for the journey northward, while John and James depart. From Phœnicia Jesus journeys along the northern borders of Galilee to Northern Decapolis,[1] and so to Bethsaida, where He is rejoined by the entire Twelve.[2] It is significant that the feeding of the four thousand, which is probably only a variant tradition of the feeding of the five thousand, is placed by Mark[3] and Matthew[4] after the journey from Sidon by way of Decapolis. The feeding of the five thousand is reported in John.[5] Andrew and Philip, representing two pairs of the Twelve, are mentioned as with him. It is also stated that "*the passover, the feast of the Jews, was at hand*,"[6] which exactly suits this time. The harmonists, even Tatian, place this event too early, and therefore find it difficult to explain the discourse of Jesus in Capernaum, which follows just after crossing the sea,[7] which offends many of His disciples and brings on the crisis in which the Twelve recognize Him distinctly as the Messiah.[8]

---

[1] Mark vii. 31. [2] Mark vi. 30 = Luke ix. 10.
[3] Mark viii. 1–9. [4] Matt. xv. 32–38.
[5] John vi. 1–15. [6] John vi. 4. [7] John vi. 16–66.
[8] John vi. 17 states that He crossed to Capernaum; Mark vi. 53, Matt. xiv. 34, to the plain of Gennesaret; Matt.

This recognition, however, according to the Synoptists, does not occur at Capernaum but at Cæsarea Philippi,[1] whither they hastened after a brief tarry at Bethsaida.[2] These rapid movements indicate a consciousness of grave peril.

This is the readjustment of the order of events in the life of Jesus which is required by the answer to the question, *Where was Jesus during the absence of the Twelve?* It solves a number of the most difficult problems of the New Testament, explains the silence of Mark as to the ministry in Peræa and Judæa, and the full report of John as to the Jerusalem ministry, and his implicit agreement with the full report of Luke

---

xv. 39 that He crossed to the borders of Magadan; Mark viii. 10 to the parts of Dalmanutha. Mark vi. 45 states that their real destination was Bethsaida. Gennesaret is a general term of the plain on the border of which Capernaum was situated. Magadan may be another name for Magdala, which is on the south side of the plain, as Capernaum is on the north. Dalmanutha may be a more precise designation of the place, which has not yet been identified. All these places were within a few miles of each other. The calm after the storm compelled them to seek the nearest land.

[1] Mark viii. 27–30; Matt. xvi. 13–20; Luke ix. 18–21.

[2] It is evident that the original plan of going to Bethsaida was carried out because of the healing of the blind man there before the journey north to Cæsarea Philippi (Mark viii. 22–26).

as to the Peræan ministry. It also fills the gap
in time which the absence of ten of the Twelve
requires by a sufficient amount of active ministry
of Jesus to satisfy all conditions of the problem.
It also explains the movements of Jesus in accordance with the perils of His position, and
enables us to see how the crisis is brought on
which finally removes every reason for caution
and justifies Him in making a distinct announcement of His Messiahship. Thus He secures His
definite acceptance as Messiah by His chief disciples, and is enabled to give them a clear warning of His impending death and resurrection just
before He makes His last journey to Jerusalem,
to the cross and the crown.

V

HOW MANY AND WHAT FEASTS DID JESUS ATTEND?

THE Synoptists mention only one feast which Jesus attended, the Passover, in connection with which He was crucified. John's Gospel also mentions this Passover, but there is a grave difference between John and the Synoptists as to the day of the crucifixion, whether it occurred on the day of the Passover, or the day before. The discussion of this difference I shall reserve for the present.

It may also be said that another earlier Passover is implied in the story of the plucking and eating ripe grain.[1] The public ministry of Jesus according to the Synoptists might thus be embraced in a period of a little more than a year.

But the Gospel of John mentions several feasts :

1. Passover, John ii. 13.
2. A feast unnamed, John v. 1.
3. Passover, John vi. 4.

---

[1] Mark ii. 23–28 ; Luke vi. 1–5 ; Matt. xii. 1–8. See p. 14.

4. Tabernacles, John vii. 2.

5. Dedication, John x. 22.

6. Passover, John xi. 55.

If the narrative of John be chronological, we have three Passovers defined, which gives us a ministry of two years and upward. The feast undefined [1] is regarded as a Passover by Robinson. This would make a ministry of three years and upward. But though a pupil of Robinson and his successor, following him for many years in this opinion, I can no longer hold it. All the other feasts are defined in this Gospel. We might say that the author who left this feast undefined most probably did not know which one it was. The argument of Robinson is based on the Hebrew usage of making the noun definite by the construct relation which is represented in Greek by the genitive. [2] This usage must be recognized as a possibility; but it is by no means certain in this case. The Sinaitic codex of the Gospel gives the definite article with the principal noun. But this cannot be given much weight over against the absence of the article in the other great Uncials of the New Testament.

---

[1] John v. 1.   [2] Robinson's *Harmony,* pp. 190 *seq.*

But even if we had sufficient evidence that this feast was made definite by the article, it by no means follows that it was the Passover. All the examples given by Robinson in which *the feast* refers to the Passover are in a context in which the Passover had been already mentioned. He gives no example in which *the feast*, at the beginning of a narrative, by itself, stands for the Passover; and even if a few instances could be given, it would not prove that it must always be so, or that it was certainly so in this particular case. It is true that Irenæus, Eusebius, Theodoret, and other early writers held that this feast was a Passover. But Tatian, Jerome, Cyril, Chrysostom held it to be Pentecost, and so Erasmus, Calvin, Beza, Bengel, and others. The feast of Purim was first suggested by Kepler, who has been followed by many modern scholars such as Neander, Olshausen, Tholuck, Meyer, and Lange. Under these circumstances we may say that the text does not determine the question. We must decide upon other grounds if at all. It seems to be most probable that it was Pentecost.[1]

We have now to consider the other feasts.

---

[1] See p. 25.

Can we be sure that the three Passovers mentioned were all different Passovers? Can we be
sure that the narrative of John's Gospel is chronological? Tatian did not think so, for he puts
the cleansing of the temple and the interview of
Jesus with Nicodemus at the last Passover. The
Synoptists all place the cleansing of the temple
at the last Passover, and that is for many reasons the most probable time of its occurrence.
Jesus would not have forced the issue between
Himself and the Sanhedrim, at the beginning of
His ministry in Jerusalem, when, even according
to John, He prudently postponed the crisis as
long as possible.

It is altogether improbable that this violent
and revolutionary act was repeated. The story of
the interview with Nicodemus is certainly given
in John too early in the development of the
teaching of Jesus. Moreover the narrative itself
implies many miracles.[1] But the only miracle
recorded prior to this narrative is the one at the
marriage feast at Cana, which certainly Nicodemus and the Jerusalemites had not witnessed,
and which they could only have heard of by rumor
if at all, and which therefore could not have had

---

[1] John ii. 23, iii. 2.

any great influence upon a man like Nicodemus, or have won the faith of any of the people of Jerusalem.

The interview with Nicodemus seems to have occurred at an earlier date than the last Passover, but not at so early a time as the order of John's Gospel would imply, if its order be regarded as chronological. These two incidents are placed here by the author of John's Gospel for topical reasons.

The Passover of John vi. 4, which was said to be " at hand " at the time of the Feeding of the multitude, was not a third intermediate Passover, but the last Passover ; for it was immediately after the Feeding of the multitude, and soon after this event Jesus goes up to Jerusalem to His last Passover as we have seen.[1]

Accordingly the three Passovers of John's Gospel are not different Passovers, but one and the same Passover, and thus the supposed differences between John and the Synoptic Gospels, in this respect, disappear. There were but two Passovers which Jesus attended, and His ministry may be embraced in less than two years.

The Gospel of John mentions the Feast of

---

[1] See p. 47.

Tabernacles,[1] and the Feast of Dedication.[2] The Feast of Dedication was not, to use modern ecclesiastical terms, a feast of obligation. But the Feast of Pentecost was one of the three feasts of obligation for which every pious Jew went up to Jerusalem to worship. It is improbable that Jesus would violate the Law. The unnamed Feast[3] was probably just this feast. If this be so, the Feasts recorded in John's Gospel give us a framework for the ministry of Jesus between the two Passovers—John v. 1 gives us Pentecost, John vii. 2 Tabernacles, John x. 22 Dedication. I have already shown that Mark ii. 23–28, Luke vi. 1–5, Matt. xii. 1–8, imply a Passover just past, and that Jesus probably began His ministry soon after the previous Feast of Tabernacles.[4]

We have then the following framework for the life of Jesus:

1. Tabernacles, October.
2. Passover, April.
3. Pentecost, June.
4. Tabernacles, October.
5. Dedication, December.
6. Passover, April.

---

[1] John vii. 2.   [2] John x. 22.   [3] John v. 1.   [4] See p. 16.

I have shown that the first Galilean ministry and the earlier Judæan ministry were prior to the first Passover.[1] I have also shown that the selection and the sending forth of the Twelve and all the related material of the Galilean ministry belong prior to the Jerusalem ministry, at Tabernacles and Dedication, and also prior to the Peræan ministry of Luke and John.[2] The journey to Jerusalem at Pentecost alone interrupts the Galilean ministry. I have shown that the journey through Samaria of John iv. is out of its historical order and really was subsequent to Dedication; and that Jesus then makes His last journey to Galilee, goes northward to Phœnicia, then to the Northern Decapolis, and meets His disciples at Bethsaida just prior to the Feeding of the multitudes; and that this was just before the last Passover.[3] So soon as we abandon the opinion that the order of John's Gospel is chronological, the separate incidents may all be arranged in a simple and natural harmony on the framework of the Feasts as given above.

There remains to be considered the discrepancy between John and the Synoptists as to the last Passover. Mark states that "*on the first*

---

[1] See p. 13 *seq.*   [2] See p. 21 *seq.*   [3] See p. 45.

*day of unleavened bread, when they sacrificed
the Passover,*" the disciples were instructed to
make ready to eat the Passover, and that they
made ready the Passover in the guest chamber
to which Jesus directed them.[1] The natural
implication from this is that they not only se-
cured a chamber for the Paschal meal, but also
made the sacrifice of the Paschal lamb in the
temple according to the Law, and prepared the
flesh with the unleavened bread and the bitter
herbs and the wine prescribed for the meal ; and
that therefore, when it was evening,[2] Jesus and
His disciples ate the Paschal lamb prior to the
institution of the Lord's supper.[3] Matthew[4] evidently depends upon Mark as its source ; for it
condenses the statement of Mark[5] into three
verses,[6] making it more evident that Jesus Himself selected the place of the meal.

Luke[7] tells us that it was Peter and John who
made these preparations. He probably had
another source of information as to this event
than Mark. He also puts the statement of time
in a different form. "*And the day of unleavened*

---

[1] Mark xiv. 12–16.
[3] Mark xiv. 18–25.
[5] Mark xiv. 12–16.
[7] Luke xxii. 7–13.

[2] Mark xiv. 17.
[4] Matt. xxvi. 17–36.
[6] Matt. xxvi. 17–19.

bread came, on which the Passover must be sacri-
ficed." [1]   The difficulty with these statements of
the Synoptists is that they do not altogether
conform to the law of the Passover.

That law [2] puts the sacrifice of the Passover
on the fourteenth of the first month between the
evenings, probably between three o'clock in the
afternoon and sundown. The feast of unleavened
bread begins on the fifteenth of the month, and
continues for a week until the twenty-first. The
first day was a great sabbath of holy convoca-
tion, the first of the seven great sabbaths, while
the seventh or last day of the Feast was the
second great sabbath. The Hebrew day began
with sunset, the fifteenth day began with night-
fall of the fourteenth, and on that evening the
Paschal lamb was eaten.   How, then, can the
Synoptists say that the Jews were accustomed
to sacrifice the Passover on the first day of unleavened bread?

It might be said that the eating of the Paschal sacrifice was on that day; but not the sacrifice itself. We might say that the author uses
sacrifice in the sense of eating of the victim.

---

[1] Luke xxii. 7.
[2] Ex. xii. 2 *seq;* Lev. xxiii. 5 ; Num. xxviii. 16 *seq.*

But then how could the preparation be made on that day? Indeed it seems rather late in a crowded city to postpone all preparations until the very day of the sacrifice. The lamb must be selected according to the Law on the tenth day, that is four days before the sacrifice.[1] This selection could hardly have been neglected. It is indeed quite possible that the casting of the traders out of the temple on the tenth day was due to an attempt to defraud His disciples in the purchase of the Paschal lamb.[2]

Dr. Robinson urges that "it was customary for the Jews, on the fourteenth day of Nisan, to cease from labor at or before midday; and to put away all leaven out of their houses before noon; and to slay the Paschal lamb toward the close of the day. Hence, in popular usage, the fourteenth day came very naturally to be reckoned as the beginning or first day of the festival;— and Josephus could say that the festival was celebrated for eight days."[3] This argument is that the Gospels are using popular rather than legal language.

This is possible and might be accepted, were

---

[1] Ex. xii. 3.   [2] See p. 103.

[3] *Harmony* Appendix Pt. VIII. iii.; Josephus *B. J.* iii. 1; *Ant.* XI. iv. 8; ii. 15. 1.

it not for the statement of the Gospel of John
which implies that Jesus did not eat the Passover
with His disciples, but was crucified on the day of
the Passover.

(1) John[1] states that the great farewell discourse of Jesus took place before the Passover.

(2) The Jews on the day of the arrest and
crucifixion " *entered not into the judgment hall
that they might not be defiled, but might eat the
Passover.*"[2] This implies that they ate the
Passover the night of the crucifixion and not before.

(3) The preparation of the Passover on the day
of crucifixion[3] implies that it was the day before
the Paschal meal.

(4) " *The preparation . . . for the day of that
sabbath was a high day,*"[4] implies the fifteenth
of Nisan, the great sabbath of the first day of
unleavened bread, on the morrow after the death
of Jesus ; and the connection of the great sabbath with the weekly sabbath.

(5) It may also be urged that the supposition
that Judas went forth just prior to the Lord's
supper to *buy what things they had need of for*

---

[1] John xiii. 1.   [2] John xviii. 28.

[3] John xix. 14.   [4] John xix. 31.

the feast,"[1] refers to the need of the Paschal
meal the next evening, and that the meeting of
the Sanhedrim to condemn Jesus was unlawful
on the sabbath and great festival days.

All this makes it evident that John represents that Jesus was crucified on the day of the
sacrifice of the Paschal lamb, and that He did
not in fact eat the Passover with His disciples,
but instituted the Lord's supper at an ordinary
meal the evening before.   This is doubtless more
suited to the conception of Jesus as Himself the
Paschal lamb, offered at the legal time; and
may also be at the basis of Paul's conception
that Jesus Himself is " *our Passover*."[2]   These
several statements of the Gospel of John are
much stronger than the single statement of the
Synoptists, which has, as we have seen, its in-
trinsic difficulties.   The error is probably in the
Synoptists. Is it a real error or only an apparent
one, and is it possible of adjustment?

Resch gives, as in the original Hebrew Gospel
upon which the Gospels depend, מקדם הפסח, which
would yield the translation, *before the Passover*.[3]
If, however, it were read בקדם, taking it as adjective, we would get the rendering : *on the first*

---

[1] John xiii. 27–30.   [2] 1 Cor. v. 7.
[3] Resch, *Die Logia Jesu*. 1898. s. 184.

day of the Passover. The variation of Luke
from Mark here is less important. The question
is as to the original of Mark. If the original
Mark was Hebrew, did it read as Delitzsch
gives it, בראשון לחג המצות, or as Resch suggests,
מקדם הפסח, or בקדם המצות, or simply קדם המצות.
The technical language is doubtless that given
by Delitzsch, but that technical language applies
to the fifteenth of the month, the day after the
sacrifice of the Passover, and could not therefore be used in popular language for the day before. It is therefore much more probable that
in the more popular language קדם would be used.
If so קדם, as written without vowel points, might
be interpreted either as a preposition, *before*,
or as an adjective, *first*. There is probably an
error of interpretation of the Hebrew Mark by the
Greek Mark at the basis of the entire difficulty.
If we interpret the original as a preposition and
render: "*before the feast of unleavened bread,
when they sacrificed the Passover, His disciples
say unto Him,*" the difficulty disappears ; for the
feast of unleavened bread is used in the general
sense as comprehending the entire Passover, as is
explained indeed by Luke;[1] and *before* that feast

---

[1] Luke xxii. 1.

is before the first event of the feast, the sacrifice
of the Paschal lamb, and therefore the day before that sacrifice, the thirteenth of Nisan.

This is confirmed by the statement of Mark [1]
that Judas arranged with the Sanhedrim to betray Jesus two days before the Passover, that is
the twelfth of Nisan. The language of Mark
would most naturally refer to the following day,
the thirteenth of Nisan, and קדם thus stands for
the day before Passover.

In this way all difficulty disappears, and we
may follow with confidence John's representation that Jesus was offered up as the Paschal
lamb on the fourteenth of Nisan, and that the
Jews celebrated the Passover meal while Jesus
was lying in the grave. Thus the statement of
John [2] that the scripture " *a bone of him shall not
be broken* " was fulfilled, in the neglect of the
soldiers to break his legs, as they did the legs of
those crucified with him ; and the statement of
St. Paul that Jesus Himself is " *our Passover*," [3]
were based on the event itself of the crucifixion
of Jesus as the Paschal sacrifice.

---

[1] Mark xiv. 1.   [2] John xix. 36.   [3] 1 Cor. v. 7.

VI

THE PERÆAN MINISTRY

THE only reference to the Peræan ministry in Mark is placed subsequent to the Galilean ministry:[1] *"And He arose from thence, and cometh into the borders of Judæa and beyond Jordan: and multitudes come together unto him again; and, as he was wont, he taught them again."* This is given in essentially the same form in Matthew.[2] It is in connection with the final journey to Jerusalem by the valley of the Jordan through Peræa. The ministry could have been but brief, a few days only. The journey corresponds with the journey reported by Luke:[3] *"And it came to pass, as they were on the way to Jerusalem, that He was passing between[4] Samaria and Galilee."* It is often identified by harmonists with the earlier journey mentioned by Luke,[5] but that is altogether improbable.

---

[1] Mark x. 1. [2] Matt. xix. 1, 2. [3] Luke xvii. 11.

[4] So Revised Version margin, which is preferred to *through the midst of* in the text.

[5] Luke ix. 51.

The material given by Mark in this connection is the following :

1. The Question of the Pharisees concerning Divorce.[1]

2. The Blessing of Little Children.[2]

3. The Counsel of Perfection.[3]

4. An Announcement of His Death and Resurrection.[4]

5. Rebuke of the Ambition of James and John.[5]

The next incident is the healing of the blind man near Jericho in Judæa. These events are in this same order in all of the Synoptists, and it is probably correct. Luke gives in addition, prior to (2) and evidently before the arrival in Peræa:

(*a*) the Healing of the Lepers,[6]

(*b*) the Discourse as to the Advent of the Kingdom,[7]

(*c*) the Parable of the Unjust Judge,[8]

(*d*) the Parable of the Pharisee and the Publican.[9]

---

[1] Mark x. 2–12 ; Matt. xix. 3–12.

[2] Mark x. 13–16 ; Matt. xix. 13–15 ; Luke xviii. 15–17.

[3] Mark x. 17–31 ; Matt. xix. 16–xx. 16 ; Luke xviii. 18–30.

[4] Mark x. 32–34 ; Matt. xx. 17–19 ; Luke xviii. 31–34.

[5] Mark x. 35–45 ; Matt. xx. 20–28.

[6] Luke xvii. 11–19.   [7] Luke xvii. 20–37.

[8] Luke xviii. 1–8.   [9] Luke xviii. 9–14.

(*a*) and (*b*) are probably in their proper place, although the greater part of the material of (*b*) is combined by Matthew xxiv. with the great eschatological discourse in Jerusalem. The two parables (*c*) and (*d*), given only by Luke, have a topical propriety here as subsequent to the question of the Pharisees as to the kingdom, and it may be that they are in their historical place. But we cannot be sure of it.

The Gospel of John, however, gives us an earlier Peræan ministry: "*And he went away again beyond Jordan into the place where John was at the first baptizing; and there he abode. And many came unto him; and they said, John indeed did no sign: but all things whatsoever John spake of this man were true. And many believed on him there.*"[1] This cannot be identified with the Peræan ministry above-mentioned. It was a prior ministry in Peræa unknown to Mark and Matthew. This ministry was subsequent to the feast of Dedication. It was from Peræa that Jesus came to Jerusalem to raise Lazarus from the dead.[2] In the above statement of John [3] the word *again* implies a visit to Peræa prior to this,

---

[1] John x. 40–42.   [2] John xi. 6, 7.
[3] John x. 40.

that is before the feast of Dedication, probably
between Tabernacles and Dedication.

When now we turn to Luke we find a Peræan
ministry of considerable extent, which may be
assigned in part to the earlier ministry suggested
by John, and in part to the later ministry stated
by John. As we have seen in a previous chapter the Seventy were sent forth on a mission to
Peræa in advance of Jesus Himself. They were
probably sent from Jerusalem after the feast
of Tabernacles. Jesus followed in their footsteps. These two ministries of Jesus in Peræa
are distinguished also in Luke, for he tells of a
journey toward Jerusalem,[1] which probably
corresponds with the journey to the feast of
Dedication. To the earlier ministry in Peræa
we may assign the greater part of what Luke
gives prior to this journey, namely :

1. The question as to prayer and the giving
of the Lord's Prayer. This was appropriate in
the scene of the Baptist's ministry, for Jesus is
asked to teach His disciples to pray as John also
taught his disciples. The incident is accompanied by an appropriate parable and a logion.[2]
The logion and the prayer are given out of place

---

[1] Luke xiii. 22.   [2] Luke xi. 1–13.

by Matthew, attached to the Sermon on the Mount.

2. The casting out of a demon from a dumb man.[1] This is given by Matthew[2] at an earlier date. But Luke's order is most probable.

This is followed by a warning against evil spirits and the sin against the Holy Spirit,[3] which is given in Mark[4] in connection with an earlier event, but evidently for topical reasons, as Mark does not give the healing of the demoniac, which is the natural basis for the discourse. This is followed in both Luke[5] and Matthew[6] by the demand for a sign and the mention of the sign of Jonah, which are given here out of place for topical reasons. It is probably the same as the demand for a sign at the close of the Galilean ministry, just before the last journey to Jerusalem, and therefore too early. Luke[7] inserts the incident of the woman pronouncing the mother of Jesus blessed, which doubtless belongs here. But Luke[8] gives a series of logia given by Matthew in part in his version of the Sermon on the

---

[1] Luke xi. 14.   [2] Matt. xii. 22, 23.
[3] Luke xi. 15–26 ; Matt. xii. 24–32, 43–45.
[4] Mark iii. 19–30.   [5] Luke xi. 29–32.
[6] Matt. xii. 38–42.   [7] Luke xi. 27, 28.
[8] Luke xi. 33–36.

Mount, and in part by Luke[1] and Mark[2] on another occasion. So also Matthew[3] gives logia not in Luke. These logia were all derived from the Logia of Matthew and are given by both evangelists in these places for topical reasons.

3. Jesus breakfasts with a Pharisee,[4] when there is a discussion as to ceremonial purification before meals; which reminds us of a similar discussion in Mark[5] and Matthew.[6] There it was the disciples who were challenged, here Jesus Himself. The former was at the close of the Galilean ministry, the latter is given by Luke here. It is possible that they are variant traditions of the same event. If so, Luke, for topical reasons, has given it out of place as an introduction to the woes pronounced against the Pharisees[7] which are given by Matthew in connection with the struggle with the Pharisees in Jerusalem in Passion week.

4. This is followed by a warning against the Pharisees,[8] which may be in place. But it is followed by a series of logia,[9] given by Matthew and Mark and even Luke himself elsewhere— thus doubtless in all cases for topical reasons.

---

[1] Luke viii. 16.   [2] Mark iv. 21.   [3] Matt. xii. 36, 37.
[4] Luke xi. 37–39.   [5] Mark vii. 1–23.   [6] Matt. xv. 1–20.
[7] Luke xi. 42–54.   [8] Luke xii. 1.   [9] Luke xii. 2–12.

5. Next comes the request of a man that Jesus may intercede with his brother as to his inheritance.[1] This is followed by the parable of the rich fool,[2] which very probably belongs here. To it are attached kindred logia,[3] given by Matthew in his version of the Sermon on the Mount, followed by parables,[4] given by Matthew in connection with the great eschatological discourse; and a series of logia[5] given by Matthew in three different connections. These are all given here for topical reasons, and have no special propriety at this time rather than another.[6]

6. The reference to the Galileans slain by Pilate in Jerusalem, with the parable of the fig tree,[7] probably belongs here.

7. The healing of the woman with an infirmity in a synagogue on the Sabbath[8] is also probably in its proper historical place. To this the parables of the grain of mustard seed and the leaven are added,[9] given by Matthew in connection with his collection of the parables of the kingdom.

All of this material is given by Luke prior to the journey to Jerusalem, which was to the

---

[1] Luke xii. 13–15.   [2] Luke xii. 16–21.   [3] Luke xii. 22–34.
[4] Luke xii. 35–48.   [5] Luke xii. 49–59.
[6] Certainly verses 35–53 seem to be too early.
[7] Luke xiii. 1–9.   [8] Luke xiii. 10–17.   [9] Luke xiii. 18–21.

feast of Dedication, according to the Gospel of John.[1]

The logia and the parables—many of them at least—were attached to the incidents for topical reasons, and do not belong there historically.

The first period of the Peræan ministry closes with the journey to the feast of Dedication.[2] To this Luke attaches logia[3] in reply to a question : " *Are they few that be saved ?* " which seem appropriate here, although given by Matthew in part in his version of the Sermon on the Mount, but in part also in several other connections.[4]

Here Luke attaches the warning given by the Pharisees against Herod, which seems quite appropriate in Peræa.[5] To this is attached a lament over Jerusalem,[6] given by Matthew[7] in Jerusalem itself, during Passion week. This lament implies several previous visits to Jerusalem and a final visit. It is out of place, therefore, in connection with a visit to the feast of Dedication followed by another visit for the raising of Lazarus before the final journey. It

---

[1] See p. 56.   [2] Luke xiii. 22.   [3] Luke xiii. 23–30.

[4] Matt. viii. 11, 12, xiii. 42, 50, xix. 30, xx. 16, xxiv. 51, xxv. 30.

[5] Luke xiii. 31–33.   [6] Luke xiii. 34, 35.

[7] Matt. xxiii. 37–39.

is equally out of place in both Matthew and Luke.

The second period of the Peræan ministry was a brief one, as it was all included in the short time between the feast of Dedication and the raising of Lazarus. The only incident mentioned probably belongs here.

1. We have first the sabbath meal with a chief Pharisee when Jesus heals a man with dropsy,[1] to which is appended the parable of the chief places at the marriage feast,[2] peculiar to Luke, with the associated logia;[3] and the parable of the marriage feast,[4] given by Matthew[5] in Passion week in Jerusalem. The connection is certainly more appropriate in Luke.

2. A series of logia,[6] spoken by Jesus to His disciples, as to counting the cost, some given by Matthew and Mark, and even Luke himself in other connections.

3. Three parables of saving the lost, in justification of His receiving sinners and eating with them, against the murmurs of the Pharisees.[7] The parable of the lost sheep is given by Mat-

---

[1] Luke xiv. 1–6.
[3] Luke xiv. 11–14.
[5] Matt. xxii. 1–10.
[7] Luke xv.

[2] Luke xiv. 7–10.
[4] Luke xiv. 15–24.
[6] Luke xiv. 25–35.

thew[1] at a later date. The other two are peculiar to Luke.

4. Then follow the parables of the shrewd steward, and of Dives and Lazarus,[2] with intervening logia, given by Matthew in his version of the Sermon on the Mount and elsewhere.

5. Next come[3] logia to the disciples, given by Matthew,[4] and Mark,[5] at a later date; and a parable peculiar to Luke. The material given here is indeed, with the single exception of the healing of the man with the dropsy, entirely teaching. Some of it is evidently out of place, although a large amount of it is quite appropriate in the connection given it by Luke.

We have sufficient evidence that the Peræan ministry was divided into three periods, and that the Seventy preceded Jesus in His work during the first period. It is probable that the Seventy continued their work until Jesus' last visit, when they joined Him for His journey to Jerusalem for the last Passover. The material given by Luke in these chapters is not in Mark, whom he follows closely in the main so far as he goes. This material is composed of: (1) Logia derived

---

[1] Matt. xviii. 12–14.   [2] Luke xvi.   [3] Luke xvii. 1–10.
[4] Matt. xviii. 6, 7, 15, 21, 22.   [5] Mark ix. 42.

from the Logia of Matthew. These logia are in Luke attached to parables and historical incidents. In Matthew's Gospel they are for the most part gathered about the four discourses—(a) The Sermon on the Mount,[1] (b) The Commission of the Twelve,[2] (c) The Woes upon the Pharisees,[3] (d) The Eschatological Discourse.[4] On the whole their location in Luke is more appropriate than in Matthew, but as we have seen, we must regard a considerable number of them as in topical rather than chronological place in Luke also.

(2) The parables may be divided into two groups, those common with Matthew and those peculiar to Luke. Those common with Matthew are given by Matthew chiefly in its groups of parables, either—(a) Parables of the kingdom, at the sea.[5] (b) In teaching the disciples.[6] (c) In conflict with the Pharisees in Jerusalem.[7] (d) Appended to the eschatological discourse.[8]

These parables are so different in Luke, in structure and detail, from the version of Matthew that it is impossible to think that they were derived from a common written source. They

---

[1] Chaps. v.–vii.   [2] Chap. x.   [3] Chap. xxiii.
[4] Chaps. xxiv., xxv.   [5] Chap. xiii.   [6] Chaps. xviii., xx.
[7] Chaps. xxi., xxii.   [8] Chaps. xxiv., xxv.

must have come from different oral sources with
varying details.   Here again the connections in
which they are given by Luke are more natural
than those in which they are given by Matthew;
although we cannot ignore the probability that
topical reasons influenced Luke also rather than
chronological reasons.

The most of the parables given by Luke in
this section are peculiar to him.   They are not
parables of the kingdom setting forth its myste-
ries.   They are parables of grace and salvation,
making plain to the people the way of salvation.
They belong to another method of teaching than
that given in Mark and Matthew.   It is altogether probable, therefore, that they belong to a
period of ministry and a place of ministry of
which Mark and Matthew knew nothing.   They
have their appropriate place in the Peræan
ministry.   In some respects their teaching is
more in accord with the Jerusalem ministry of
John than with the Galilean ministry of Mark.

(3) There are but few incidents in these chapters as compared with those giving the Galilean
ministry of Mark, and the Jerusalem ministry of
John.   The reason for this was probably the historical situation,—peril from Herod, and the
constant hostility of the Pharisees.   Jesus' minis-

try was less in the synagogues and less in public
than during the Galilean ministry.   It was more
in private and more in teaching disciples.   The
work of the Seventy was going on all through
Peræa during this period.   If they went in pairs
there were thirty-five or thirty-six different
missions which must have covered the whole
land of Peræa and much of Judæa also, at least
the whole valley of the Jordan.   There is no
sufficient reason, therefore, to think of a written
source for this material.   It was derived by
Luke from some one or more of the companions
of Jesus in this ministry; for it is altogether
probable that one of the pairs of the Twelve
continued with Him during all this period.   If
James and John, owing to their connections in
Jerusalem, remained for the most part during
this period in Jerusalem, it may well be that
they brought to Jesus the sad report of the
death of Lazarus, for John gives the narrative
and words at this time.   It may be that
Matthew and his mate Thomas were the companions of Jesus in the Peræan ministry.
Thomas is mentioned [1] as being with Jesus in
Peræa.   He it is who, when some disciples

---

[1] John xi. 16.

object to the journey to Jerusalem for the raising of Lazarus, heroically says, "*Let us also
go that we may die with him.*" No other member of the Twelve is mentioned in connection
with events or discourses which certainly belong
to the Peræan ministry. The reference to
Peter, in Luke,[1] is in connection with a parable
which is not in its local or chronological place.
Matthew was the mate of Thomas in the list of
the Twelve, so that he must have been with his
mate at this time. This explains how Matthew
in his Logia could give Peræan logia as well as
Galilean. The Logia of Matthew, if it gave any
historical incidents at all, gave them only briefly
as introductory to logia. Matthew's Gospel, as
we now have it, came from a different and a later
hand. Luke's versions of the logia are usually
nearer the original of Matthew's Logia in order, form, and substance, than the versions of
Matthew's Gospel. There are also in the parables peculiar to Luke certain characteristics
which Matthew, the publican, would have appre-
hended more than any other of the Twelve.
And it is quite possible that Luke had received
oral information from Matthew himself. How-

---

[1] Luke xii. 41.

ever this may be, the sources of Luke for the
Peræan ministry were reliable oral sources, and
when the material is properly arranged, it fits
into the Life of Jesus with nicety and floods it
with light.

VII

JESUS AND THE PHARISEES

THE Pharisees were the dominant party in Judaism in the time of Jesus. Party spirit prevailed to an extraordinary degree, not only against their chief antagonists, the Sadducees, who had possession of the chief places of the priesthood, and great political influence; but also against the minor parties such as the Herodians and Essenes, and indeed between the Pharisee schools of Hillel and Shammai.[1] It was only natural, therefore, that they should look with suspicion upon the rise of a new party, at first under the leadership of the Baptist and then under the headship of Jesus. The Gospel of Matthew[2] represents that the Baptist sharply rebuked the Pharisees and Sadducees who came to his baptism. This is, however, not given in Mark, and Luke gives the rebuke a more general reference to the multitude.[3] The Gospel of

---

[1] See *Messiah of the Gospels*, pp. 38 *seq.*
[2] Matt. iii. 7–10.   Matt. iii. 7–9.

John states that the Pharisees sent representatives from Jerusalem to the Baptist to inquire who he was and why he baptized.[1]

The first conflict between Jesus and the Pharisees, according to Mark, was in Capernaum during the introductory Galilean ministry. They accused Him of blasphemy because He said to the man sick of the palsy, " *Thy sins are forgiven*," and because of His asserting His authority as the Son of Man to forgive sins.[2]

They next accused Him of associating with publicans and sinners, because, after calling Matthew to be His disciple, He was present at a farewell feast given by Matthew to his friends.[3] A third conflict soon followed as to fasting, in which Jesus defended the action of His disciples, in not conforming to the uses of the Pharisees in this respect.[4] It is probable also that the discussion as to purification, about the same time, was one in which the Pharisees took an active part.[5] If all these disputes had already taken place in Galilee and in the valley of the Jordan

---

[1] John i. 19–28.
[2] Mark ii. 1–12 ; Matt. ix. 2–8 ; Luke v. 17–26.
[3] Mark ii. 13–17 ; Matt. ix. 9–13 ; Luke v. 27–32.
[4] Mark ii. 18–22 ; Matt. ix. 14–17 ; Luke v. 33–39.
[5] John iii. 25.

before Passover, we can understand that the jealousy of the Pharisees at the greater success of Jesus than of John in winning disciples may have been so strong that it was prudent of Jesus, immediately after Passover, to depart to Galilee.[1]

On the way to Galilee another and still more serious conflict arose respecting the Sabbath, which became, from this time on, the most serious question in debate.   Jesus and His disciples were charged with violating the Sabbath because He allowed His disciples to pluck from the standing grain and eat it.[2] This is followed, in the narratives, by His healing the man with a withered hand on the sabbath.[3] It is evident that the Pharisees were already excited against Him on this occasion. They were watching Him for an opportunity to accuse Him. And after this cure they took counsel with the Herodians to destroy Him. These two incidents are put together by the evangelists. But it is probable that this order was for topical reasons, and that the second incident was some time later. For the plotting of the Pharisees and the

---

[1] John iv. 1–3.
[2] Mark ii. 23–28 ; Matt. xii. 1–8 ; Luke vi. 1–5.
[3] Mark iii. 1–6 ; Matt. xii. 9–14 ; Luke vi. 6–11.

Herodians at so early a date would have made
His second Galilean ministry more difficult than
it appears to have been from the narratives of
this period.   If the order of events given in
previous chapters is correct, the last incident
is probably the climax of the opposition of the
Pharisees, before He goes up to Jerusalem to
the feast of Pentecost.

At this feast Jesus heals an infirm man on the
sabbath.[1]   The Pharisees of Jerusalem, therefore, are now stirred up against Him for violating, as they supposed, the law of the sabbath.
He claims the authority to do this miracle on
the sabbath as the Son of the Father, and so
another ground of controversy arises respecting
His claim of a special Sonship to God.   Luke [2]
gives a touching story of Jesus at a meal in the
house of a Pharisee, allowing a magdalene to
kiss His feet, and then of His absolving her from
all her sins.   Whether this occurred in the second Galilean ministry, or at the beginning of the
third, it is not easy to determine.   It combines
two grounds of accusation already given in other
connections apart, namely, contact with sinners
and His pronouncing forgiveness of sins.   The

---

[1] John v. 1–18.   [2] Luke vii. 36–50.

situation is, however, less serious than that reported in connection with the sabbath cure,[1] and on that account might seem earlier. But, on the other hand, a different place at a later date might show a less serious situation. This is, as I understand it, the sum of the conflicts of Jesus with the Pharisees during His Galilean ministry.

The scene now shifts to Jerusalem, where the conflict becomes much more serious, beginning with a reference back to the healing of the infirm man already considered.[2] This conflict broke out afresh at the feast of Tabernacles. John[3] reports a continuous discussion with the Pharisees in which Jesus is in constant peril of His life. It is probable that the most of this material belongs to a later date. The only event mentioned is the healing on the sabbath, of the man born blind, with the discussion based upon it.[4] As Jesus' discourse on the last or great day of the feast is given[5] previously, we must either suppose that Jesus remained in Jerusalem some time after the conclusion of the feast day, in which the material of John must be placed ; or if Jesus departed from Jerusalem on His Peræan

---

[1] Mark iii. 1–6.
[2] John vii. 19–24.
[3] John vii.–x. 21.
[4] John ix.
[5] John vii. 37–52.

ministry directly after the feast, the material of
these chapters must be put at another and later
time. The latter opinion is more probable.
The word of Jesus as to His pre-existence [1]
seems to be too early. And the same may be
said of the crisis connected with the healing of
the blind man.[2] In fact this material should be
attached to the visit to Jerusalem at the feast of
Dedication.

We next turn our attention to the Peræan
ministry, where the conflict with the Pharisees
enters upon another stage. In the first Peræan
ministry the conflict begins with the healing of
a demoniac. The Pharisees charge Jesus with
casting out demons through the authority of the
prince of demons. Jesus warns them of the sin
against the Divine Spirit.[3] The logia attached
are given by Mark[4] in connection with another
incident in Galilee. But this conflict is without
sufficient motive in Mark at so early a date. It
is appropriate where Luke puts it after the conflict already considered. The next contest is at
the table of a Pharisee, with reference to ceremonial purification before meals.[5] A similar dis-

---

[1] John viii. 56–59.   [2] John ix.

[3] Luke xi. 14–15 ; Matt. xii. 22–24.

[4] Mark iii. 22–30.   [5] Luke xi. 37–41.

cussion is given in Mark.[1] It is possible that
these are different reports of one and the same
discussion, especially as Luke does not report
the story of Mark, and Mark does not give the
story of Luke, while Matthew follows Mark. It
is also possible, however, that this discussion
may have occurred twice, because the stories are
altogether different. The agreement is only in
the essential subject of controversy. If the
former alternative be correct, we must regard its
place here in Luke as due to topical considerations, although it must be recognized that he
gives it a better setting. To this incident Luke
attaches a series of woes upon the Pharisees[2]
given by Matthew in connection with the final
struggle in Jerusalem.[3] The connection of Luke
has topical propriety, but it is improbable that
Jesus would have uttered these woes at the table
of a Pharisee where He was a guest. They are
derived by both Matthew and Luke from the
Logia of Matthew, where they probably had no
historical connection. Each evangelist gives
them in a connection most appropriate topically
according to his mind. Matthew's use of them

---

[1] Mark vii. 1–23 ; Matt. xv. 1–20.   [2] Luke xi. 42–52.
[3] Matt. xxiii.

seems on the whole more appropriate. They
apply, many of them, to the Pharisees of Jerusalem rather than to those of Peræa. The
warnings against the leaven of the Pharisees [1] is
appropriate in this connection and may be in its
proper place, although it is given in Mark [2] in a
still more appropriate place later. Luke [3] reports the healing of a woman on the Sabbath
with the usual opposition of the Pharisees, here
represented by the ruler of the synagogue.

Jesus now returns to Jerusalem to the feast
of Dedication. For what reason Jesus went up
thither we are not informed. He probably had
prudential reasons, as He had to steer between
the Scylla of Herod and the Charybdis of the
Sanhedrim at this time. All that is reported at
this feast is given in John x. 22–39. This is too
meagre to explain this journey. It is altogether
probable, therefore, that the incidents reported
in the previous chapter of John belong here. [4]
It is probable also, that the healing of the
blind man on the sabbath occurred at this time.
We may then explain the intensity of the hos-

---

[1] Luke xii. 1.   [2] Mark viii. 15 ; Matt. xvi. 6.

[3] Luke xiii. 10–17.

[4] John x. 26–29 implies x. 1–21 ; and x. 29–39 implies viii.
12–59.

tility of the Pharisees in view of the assertion of
Jesus of His pre-existence as the Son of the
Father, and His assertion of His Messiahship.
No wonder that His life was now in extreme
peril and that He had to depart again to Peræa.

The second Peræan ministry renews the conflict with the Pharisees. Another sabbath meal
with a Pharisee, when Jesus heals the man with
the dropsy,[1] renews the discussion as to the sabbath. Receiving and eating with sinners, against
which the Pharisees murmured, is the occasion
of the three parables of salvation.[2] The rebuke
of the Pharisaic love of money is given in two
other parables.[3] Jesus now suddenly goes up to
Jerusalem to raise Lazarus from the dead.[4] His
disciples remonstrate with Him because of the
extreme peril of such a course. Thomas alone
of the Twelve is mentioned as present. He is
mated with Matthew in the lists of the six
pairs of the Twelve, who was probably present
also.

The conflict has now reached its crisis in Jerusalem, and the Pharisees in council, under the
advice of Caiaphas, the Sadducee high-priest,

---

[1] Luke xiv. 1–6.   [2] Luke xv.   [3] Luke xvi.
[4] John xi.

decide to put Jesus to death. So Jesus hastily departed from Jerusalem to Ephraim. After a brief tarrying there, He journeys northward through Samaria, and secretly through Galilee to Phœnicia, then on the border of Galilee and Syria, to Decapolis, where the final Galilean ministry begins. The conflict with the Pharisees in Galilee now becomes much sharper. They persist in demanding a sign and stir up the people to this demand. This is evident in the discourse in the synagogue of Capernaum,[1] which is probably the same incident as that briefly given in another connection in Mark.[2] Here comes the sign of the prophet Jonah, which is the symbol of His death and resurrection. This is appropriately followed by the warning against the leaven of the Pharisees.[3] It is probable that the discussion as to ceremonial purification before meals[4] belongs here, with the rebuke of the Pharisees for making void the word of God by their traditions.

Jesus now leaves Galilee on His last journey to Jerusalem, passing through Peræa. On this journey comes the question of the Pharisees con-

---

[1] John vi. 26–40.   [2] Mark viii. 10–13 ; Matt. xvi. 1–4.

[3] Mark viii. 14–21 ; Matt. xvi. 5–12.

[4] Mark vii. 1–23 ; Matt. xv. 1–20.

cerning divorce,[1] the discourse with the Pharisees
as to the advent of the kingdom, with the eschatological discourse attached,[2] and the parable
of the Pharisee and the Publican.[3]

Jesus now enters Jerusalem, and the last struggle begins. This was a battle of words between
Jesus and the Pharisees, in which, however, the
other parties join. It probably lasted two days,
in which Jesus finally silences all His adversaries.
The report is given by Mark.[4] Luke[5] follows
Mark closely, omitting, however, the question as
to the great commandment,[6] which is given by
him in another connection, and in another
form.[7] Matthew[8] greatly enlarges the material
not only by the addition of parables, given by
Luke elsewhere, but also by the heaping up of
woes upon the Pharisees, given by Luke as we
have seen in connection with the Peræan ministry. The connection of Matthew seems more
appropriate, but we cannot be sure that these
logia are not indeed a gathering up of logia
spoken on many different occasions. The con-

---

[1] Mark x. 2–12 ; Matt. xix. 3–12.
[2] Luke xvii. 20–37.   [3] Luke xviii. 9–14.
[4] Mark xi. 27–xii. 41.   [5] Luke xx. 1–47.
[6] Mark xii. 28–34 ; Matt. xxii. 34–40.
[7] Luke x. 25–37.   [8] Matt. xxi. 23–xxiii.

flict with the Pharisees had reached its goal.
The Sanhedrim, controlled by the Pharisees, had
determined His death.   The grounds of accusation had been prepared.   But Jesus makes all
this unnecessary, for under oath before the Sanhedrim He meets the essential issue, asserts distinctly that He is the Messiah, is condemned
for blasphemy on that account, and is given over
to Herod to be crucified as King of the Jews.

VIII

WHEN DID JESUS FIRST DECLARE HIS MESSIAHSHIP?

ANY attempt to harmonize the Gospels on the basis of a chronological order of the material in Mark or John is wrecked upon insuperable obstacles. None of these is more important than the Messianic claims of Jesus. It is evident from the Synoptists that His claims were for the greater part of His Galilean ministry veiled behind the term Son of Man; and from the Gospel of John in the Jerusalem ministry, behind the term Son of the Father.[1] But there comes a time when Jesus distinctly claims recognition as the Messiah, and indeed as the suffering Messiah. If we could find an adequate reason for this change of policy, and fix the time of the change, one of the most important problems in the life of Jesus would be solved.

Such a reason and such a date are given in the story, John xi. 47–54. The Sanhedrim followed

---

[1] *The Incarnation of our Lord*, pp. 28 *seq.*, 50 *seq.*

the advice of the chief priest Caiaphas, and de
cided upon the death of Jesus as the only way in
which to save the nation. This was soon after
the resurrection of Lazarus—not long after the
feast of Dedication, probably at the close of December, or the beginning of January. This decision of the Sanhedrim made the arrest and
death of Jesus only a question of time and of
opportunity. Jesus was at once informed of
this decision and—"*therefore walked no more
openly among the Jews, but departed thence into
the country near to the wilderness, into a city
called Ephraim ; and there He tarried with the
disciples.*"[1] It became evident, therefore, that
the next time Jesus appeared in Jerusalem
He would meet His arrest and death. And it
was not at all improbable that the Sanhedrim
would send officers after Him to arrest Him on
His journey. The little city of Ephraim on the
borders of the wilderness and of Samaria afforded
Him an easy and speedy way of escape from
such a pursuit. There was now, therefore, no
longer any reason for reticence as to His Messiahship on the part of Jesus. His enemies had
decided upon His death.

---

[1] John xi. 54.

Indeed we may go back to the feast of Dedication for the beginning of this critical situation. He went up to that feast from Peræa to escape Herod and to continue His conflict with the Pharisees in Jerusalem. It was at this feast that He first advanced His Messianic relation as the Son of the Father to the assertion of His pre-existence before Abraham, and only escaped stoning for blasphemy by hurried escape from the Temple. It was at this feast that He distinctly asserted His Messiahship to the blind man He had healed, and claimed his allegiance. The Messianic claims of Jesus, therefore, were brought clearly before the Sanhedrim and the people of Jerusalem. They themselves had forced the issue. They must either accept Jesus or reject Him. They determined to reject Him as a blaspheming pretender, and to expel the blind man, whom Jesus had healed, from the synagogue, as His disciple. This was the beginning of the policy of active persecution of Jesus and His disciples. Jesus, when he went up to Jerusalem to the raising of Lazarus, knew that He was entering into greater peril than He was exposed to from Herod in Peræa. His disciples interposed with an objection to the journey, but in vain.

His death was decreed by the Sanhedrim at the feast of Dedication. It was certain to take place when next He came to Jerusalem at the ensuing Passover. There remained only about four months [1] during which He could secure from His disciples the recognition of His Messiahship, and therefore the time had come for Him to make this the burden of His teaching. After a brief sojourn in Ephraim Jesus makes the journey through Samaria to Galilee. In Samaria He was safe from the Sanhedrim and from Herod. At Sychar, the ancient seat of Jacob's well, He distinctly claims to be the Messiah and accepts the recognition of the Samaritans. [2] The narrative tells us that He abode with them two days. On entering Galilee, He goes to Nazareth, His birthplace, and in the synagogue on the Sabbath, declares that He is the Messianic prophet of the second Isaiah, and gives His native city an opportunity of recognizing Him, which, however, His townsmen refused; and with difficulty He escapes their hands. [3] He thus realizes His peril, not only from Herod, but from the people of Galilee, even from those

---

[1] John iv. 35.   [2] John iv. 25, 26.
[3] Luke iv. 16–30 ; Mark vi. 1–6 ; Matt. xiii. 54–58.

whom He had a right to expect would be most favorable to Him.

Accordingly He at once departs to Phœnicia to the borders of Tyre and Sidon, Peter and Andrew probably being His only companions. Even there He wished to remain unknown.[1] From thence He journeys along the northern borders of Galilee through the midst of the borders of Decapolis (the northern section), and goes up into a mountain, not far from Bethsaida,[2] which belonged to the jurisdiction of Philip. Here the Twelve join Him. But a great multitude crowd to Him also, and He works many cures and feeds the multitude in the wilderness. He sends the Twelve by sea to Bethsaida, while He Himself remains behind and apart to pray.[3] A storm forces the Twelve out of their course, and Jesus comes to them walking on the sea.[4] A calm coming on they are compelled to land in the plain of Gennesaret instead of at Bethsaida, and probably near Magdala at its southern end.[5] Jesus crosses the plain to Capernaum, where He delivers the discourse in the synagogue which brings on a crisis among His disciples. Many of His disciples abandon

---

[1] Mark vii. 24.   [2] Mark vii. 31–37; Matt. xv. 29–31.
[3] Mark vi. 45, 46.   [4] Mark vi. 47–56.
[5] See p. 48.

Him, but the Twelve remain faithful, and
speaking through Peter recognize Him as the
Messiah.[1] This recognition is placed in John at
the close of the discourse; but it is doubtless the
same recognition as that given by the Synoptists
a little later at Cæsarea Philippi.[2]

The demand for a sign[3] other than His
miracles is probably the same as that given in
the Synoptists,[4] in which, under the symbol of
Jonah, Jesus gives a veiled prediction of His
death and resurrection.

He crosses again to the other side of the sea,[5]
doubtless for prudential reasons, and goes to
Bethsaida with the Twelve, where He heals a
blind man,[6] and then journeys rapidly northward
to Cæsarea Philippi, at the base of Hermon,
where Peter, as the spokesman of the Twelve,
distinctly recognizes Him as the Messiah.[7] Jesus
then tells them of His impending death and
resurrection.[8] This is followed by the Transfiguration.[9] The grand tone of all His conversa-

---

[1] John vi. 22–71.   [2] See p. 47.

[3] John vi. 30.   [4] Mark viii. 11, 12; Matt. xvi. 1–4.

[5] Mark viii. 13.   [6] Mark viii. 22–26.

[7] Mark viii. 27–30; Matt. xvi. 13–20; Luke ix. 18–21.

[8] Mark viii. 31–ix. 1; Luke ix. 22–27; Matt. xvi. 21–28.

[9] Mark ix. 2–13; Matt. xvii. 1–13; Luke ix. 28–36.

tions with His disciples subsequent to this event
is His impending death.[1]

How natural all this is if it occurred a few
days before His death, which He knew to have
been already decided upon by the Sanhedrim.
His journeys up to this time must have con-
sumed several weeks. John[2] states that the
Passover was at hand. We may therefore conclude that the month of Nisan was about to
begin at the time of the feeding of the multitudes. He must have been, therefore, within less
than three weeks of His death when at Cæsarea
Philippi. How unnatural it is if all this is
placed in the middle of His ministry, a year or
more before His death, as the harmonists are
accustomed to arrange it.

From Cæsarea Philippi, Jesus with the Twelve
returns to Capernaum,[3] on a rapid journey to
Jerusalem. He now takes the usual route, by
the valley of the Jordan, followed by His disciples and the multitudes. He crosses to Peræa,[4]
where it is probable that the Seventy rejoin
Him. Then He continues His journey up to
Jerusalem,[5] accompanied by both the Twelve

---

[1] Mark ix. 9–13, 30–32.   [2] John vi. 4.
[3] Mark ix. 33; Matt. xvii. 24.   [4] Mark x. 1.
[5] Mark x. 32–45.

and the Seventy; and again foretells to the
Twelve His impending death and gives the high
calling to suffer martyrdom in like manner. At
Jericho, where the journey was naturally inter-
rupted for a rest, He heals a blind man,[1] and
accepts Zacchæus as a disciple, with whom He
lodges for a night.[2] He then journeys on to
Jerusalem, arriving at Bethany six days before
the beginning of Passover,[3] late Friday on the
evening beginning Sabbath. He lodges with
Lazarus over Sabbath, and is anointed by Mary
at a supper on the Sabbath. This which was
designed by her in His honor, but was interpreted by Jesus as for His burial, was indeed
the provocation for the betrayal of Judas. Passion week has begun.

The next day, Sunday, the ninth of Nisan, He
enters Jerusalem accompanied by the Twelve
and the Seventy and a great throng of His disciples, and He accepts their enthusiastic recognition of Him as the Messiah.[4] He knows
He is about to die. There is no longer reason
for hesitation. The more public the better.
Jerusalem must accept Him or reject Him.

---

[1] Mark x. 46-52.

[2] Luke xix. 1-10.

[3] John xii. 1-8.

[4] Mark xi. 1-11.

This was her last opportunity. The casting out of the traders from the temple on the tenth was a still more marked declaration of His Messianic authority. A few days of conflict with the Pharisees, Sadducees, and Herodians, in which all these parties tried to entrap Him and get from Him grounds for condemnation—a few days of struggle between the Galilean and Peræan multitudes who followed Him and the crowds of Jerusalem who rejected Him—a few more days for the instruction of His disciples—the case against Him had been prepared and was ready; it was only necessary to arrest Him with as little disturbance as possible; the treachery of Judas enabled the Sanhedrim to make a quiet arrest in the night, and to hurry forward the process against Him, declare Him guilty, and secure the consent of the Roman Governor to His crucifixion, just before the Passover feast began.

The order of events given above is a natural order—it is an order that exhibits a rapid development of events rushing on to the crisis, and it avoids the inconsistencies of the premature declaration and recognition of His Messiahship, and especially of a prediction of His death, months before there was any real peril of it, which the ordinary arrangement of the material gives us. Such a view, indeed, enhances the predictive element in the discourses of Jesus, but on the other hand it is difficult to see any real occasion for such prediction at so early a stage in His career, and it results in an apparently unnecessary and premature puzzling of His disciples with new difficulties, when those they were compelled to confront were great enough and severe enough in any case.

IX

THE ORDER OF EVENTS IN PASSION WEEK

THE Gospels heap up events and discourses in the last week of Jesus' life. There are several difficult problems connected with the arrangement of the material. The Gospel of John tells us[1] that Jesus came to Bethany six days before the Passover. This statement seems definite enough, and yet there are three different opinions as to the day, whether it was Friday, Saturday, or Sunday. This statement of the Gospel of John must be interpreted in accordance with the subsequent statement of this Gospel as to the Passover. As we have seen, John represents the crucifixion as taking place at the time of the sacrifice of the Passover on Friday, the fourteenth of Nisan—six days before would give us Saturday the eighth. Jesus having made the journey from Jericho on Friday, arrives late in the day on the evening after the Sabbath had begun. The Sabbath would then be spent in Bethany. This

---

[1] John xii. 1.

gives room for the supper at Bethany on the Sabbath.

The Sabbath seems to have been the customary time for social gatherings in the time of Jesus. In John it is directly attached to the arrival in Bethany,[1] and gives a proper opportunity for the coming of the crowds to see Jesus and Lazarus.[2] Another account of this supper and of the anointing is given in the Synoptists,[3] subsequent to the statement that the Sanhedrim two days before the Passover decided to betray Him. But this is doubtless a topical order due to the fact that the waste of this anointing is given as the motive for the betrayal of Judas,[4] which naturally comes after the determination to put Jesus to death. We may therefore follow John rather than Mark as to the time of the anointing, all the more that it gives Judas time to brood over his dissatisfaction before he finally decides to become a traitor.

John[5] tells us that on the morrow, that is Sunday, the ninth of Nisan, Jesus made His Messianic entry into Jerusalem. The Synop-

[1] John xii. 2–8. [2] John xii. 9–11.
[3] Mark xiv. 3–9; Matt. xxvi. 6–13. [4] Mark xiv. 10, 11.
[5] John xii. 12–19.

tists [1] give it in connection with the journey from Jericho, so that it seems as if He went right on into Jerusalem the same day. The statement of John is more natural and so more probable. In the evening He retires to Bethany with the Twelve.[2]

On the morrow, that is Monday, the tenth of Nisan,[3] on His way to the temple, Jesus cursed the fig tree, and on His entry into the temple, cast out the traders because they had made it a den of thieves.[4] As the tenth day was the day of selecting the paschal lamb, it is quite possible that an attempt to defraud Jesus and His disciples in the purchase of the lamb excited His indignation and induced Him to this assertion of His Messianic authority. Again He went forth to Bethany and lodged there.[5] Luke tells us, however, that He went to the Mount of Olives. And it may be that Jesus and His disciples lodged in the open air rather than in houses.

In the morning, that is Tuesday, the eleventh of Nisan, they passed by the fig tree and found it withered away from the roots.[6] Now begins

---

[1] Mark xi. 1–11 ; Luke xix. 29–44 ; Matt. xxi. 1–11.

[2] Mark xi. 11.   [3] Mark xi. 12–14 ; Matt. xviii. 18, 19.

[4] Mark xi. 15–19 ; Matt. xxi. 12–17 ; Luke xix. 45–48.

[5] Matt. xxi. 17.   [6] Mark xi. 20–25 ; Matt. xxi. 20–22.

the conflict of Jesus with the Pharisees and
other Jewish sects, who try one after the other
to entrap Him. The Synoptists begin the narrative immediately after the narrative of the
withering of the fig tree but without any precise indication of time: *"And they come again
to Jerusalem;"* [1] *"and when he was come into
the temple;"* [2] Luke [3] makes the statement,
"And it came to pass, on one of the days."
This is preceded by the general statement, [4]
*"And he was teaching daily in the temple.
But the chief priests and the scribes and the
principal men of the people sought to destroy
him; and they could not find what they might
do; for the people all hung upon him, listen-
ing."* [5] It is probable, therefore, that we have
to distribute these discussions over two days,
Tuesday and Wednesday. It is evident that
a large amount of additional material given here
by Matthew is used in accordance with his
method of gathering logia, parables, and discussions spoken on different occasions in connection with some principal occasion. Much of
this is given on other occasions in the other

---

[1] Mark xi. 27.   [2] Matt. xxi. 23.

[3] Luke xx. 1.   [4] Luke xix. 47, 48.

[5] Mark xi. 18.

Gospels. Mark, supported by Luke and John, are therefore the only safe guides. The first and most natural question is as to Jesus' authority.[1] This was probably on Tuesday, the day after His expulsion of the traders from the temple. This is followed by a parable of the wicked husbandmen,[2] to which Matthew has attached two other similar parables.[3]

It is probable that we must assign the questions [4] to the next day, Wednesday, the twelfth of Nisan, for they are represented as put to Him in the execution of a plan which had been determined upon after careful deliberation.[5] The questions were designed to ensnare Him. Three different parties came to Him for this purpose— (1) the Herodians,[6] who try to entrap Him in a question as to the lawfulness of paying tribute to Cæsar. (2) Next the Sadducees test Him as to the Resurrection.[7] (3) Finally the Pharisees test Him as to the Law.[8] Jesus now turns

---

[1] Mark xi. 27–33 ; Matt. xxi. 23–27 ; Luke xx. 1–8.
[2] Mark xii. 1–12 ; Luke xx. 9–19.
[3] Matt. xxi. 28–41 ; xxii. 1–14.
[4] Mark xii. 13–34 ; Matt. xxii. 15–40; Luke xx. 20–40.
[5] Mark xii. 13 ; Matt. xxii. 15 ; Luke xx. 20.
[6] Mark xii. 13–17 ; Matt. xxii. 16–22; Luke xx. 21–26.
[7] Mark xii. 18–27 ; Matt. xxii. 23–33 ; Luke xii. 27–40.
[8] Mark xii. 28–34 ; Matt. xxii. 34–40.

the tables on them with a question as to the
Messiah,[1] which they cannot answer, and concludes with an exposure of the hypocrisy of the
Pharisees,[2] to which Matthew adds a large
amount of material from earlier occasions.[3]   It
is probable that the story of the widow's mite [4]
belongs to this day, and at its close the Eschatological discourse to the disciples on the mount
of Olives,[5] to which Matthew has added a large
amount of additional material,[6] a considerable
portion of which is given by Luke elsewhere.
Matthew indeed puts this discourse two days
before the Passover.   Matthew [7] and Mark [8] tell
us that it was on this day, two days before the
Passover, that the Sanhedrim decided to put
Jesus to death.   They decided to take Him by
craft and not during the feast, in order to avoid
a tumult among the people.   It is probable
that. Judas came to them and arranged for the
betrayal at this time, although it is quite possible that it was not until the following day.[9]

---

[1] Mark xii. 35–37; Matt. xxii. 41–46; Luke xx. 41–44.

[2] Mark xii. 38–40; Luke xx. 45–47.   [3] Matt. xxiii.

[4] Mark xii. 41–44; Luke xxi. 1–4.

[5] Mark xiii.; Luke xxi. 5–38.   [6] Matt. xxiv–xxv.

[7] Matt. xxvi. 1, 2.   [8] Mark xiv. 1–2.

[9] Mark xiv. 10, 11; Luke xxii. 3–5; Matt. xxvi. 14–16.

The day before the Passover had now come. What shall we assign to that day? Did Jesus remain on the Mount of Olives apart by Himself, or did He go again to the temple? In the latter case are we to place any of the discussions given above so late? This is improbable. The contest of words had reached its end. His opponents had been so defeated that they had given up the contest and only now thought of His arrest and death. It is quite possible that Jesus spent this day in retirement, so far as the morning and afternoon were concerned. But it is more probable that He used it for a final discourse in the temple. The Gospel of John indeed gives us material which comes in appropriately here, and which it is difficult to put on an earlier day. John [1] tells us of a meeting with some Greeks in the temple, a theophany there, a declaration of His death, and a final rejection by the people, and ends with the statement—"*He departed and hid himself from them.*"

If the interpretation [2] given in a previous chapter is correct, on this day Jesus sends Peter and John to prepare for the Passover meal. The story implies secrecy as to the place. On the

---

[1] John xii. 20–36.

[2] Mark xiv. 12; Luke xxii. 7; Matt. xxvi. 17. See pp. 61 *seq.*

evening after the close of this day, on Friday, the fourteenth of Nisan, Jesus holds His farewell meal with the Twelve, and institutes the Lord's supper,[1] which is connected with a long farewell discourse of John.[2]

In the night they go forth to Gethsemane at the foot of the Mount of Olives, where He undergoes the agony of His last preparation for martyrdom.[3] Then follows His betrayal by Judas, His arrest by the officers of the Sanhedrim, and His interrogation and trial before the Sanhedrim, all of which occurred during the night. On the morning of Friday, the fourteenth of Nisan, the Sanhedrim accuse Him before Pilate and demand His death. Pilate examines Him and can find no fault in Him. Desirous of pleasing the Jews, he offers them the choice of Jesus or Barabbas. They choose Barabbas and demand the crucifixion of Jesus. Pilate complies with their demand. Jesus is mocked as King of the Jews, is scourged by the soldiers of Herod and Pilate, and taken off to be crucified. During the extremity of His agony,

---

[1] Mark xiv. 12–26 ; Matt. xxvi. 17–36 ; Luke xxii. 7–30.

[2] Chaps. xiii.–xvii.

[3] Mark xiv. 32–42 ; Matt. xxvi. 36–46 ; Luke xxii. 39–46 ; John xviii. 1.

from the sixth to the ninth hour, from midday to three o'clock in the afternoon, there was an eclipse of the sun and an earthquake. Jesus seems to have expired about three o'clock in the afternoon, at the time when it was usual to begin the sacrifice of the Paschal lamb in the temple. The veil of the temple was rent by the earthquake, to show that it was now abandoned by God. The true Paschal lamb had just been sacrificed, the animal victims were no longer of any value.

The time for the eating of the Passover was rapidly approaching, and it was improper to allow the bodies to remain on the cross; for that would desecrate the feast. Accordingly they were removed in great haste after death had been certified. Joseph of Arimathæa obtained from Pilate authority to remove the body of Jesus to his own tomb. He was assisted by Nicodemus and the women from Galilee in the preparation of the body for entombment.

On the Sabbath, the fifteenth of Nisan, Jesus remained in the tomb. But on Sunday, the sixteenth of Nisan, the day of the Omer offering, He arose from the dead according to His promise and showed Himself to His disciples during forty days, after which He ascended to His heavenly throne to reign as the Messianic King.

X

THE FORTY DAYS OF THE RISEN JESUS

THE earliest written reference to the resurrection of Jesus is in the Epistle to the Galatians, written less than twenty years after the event. Paul claims to have received his Gospel by revelation from the risen Jesus.[1] The First Epistle to the Corinthians, written some five years later, makes the resurrection of Christ the cardinal principle of the Christian religion, and gives a number of appearances of the risen Jesus to His disciples.[2] These are no less than six in number : (1) to Cephas, or Peter, (2) to the Twelve, (3) to more than five hundred brethren, (4) to James, the Lord's brother, (5) to all the apostles, (6) to Paul himself. This was many years before any of the Gospels were written. In view of this full report of Paul, it is certainly surprising that the Gospel of Mark gives no account whatever of the appearances of Jesus. It is true that we have[3] an account of several appearances of the risen Jesus: (1) to Mary Mag-

---

[1] Gal. i. 11–12. [2] 1 Cor. xv. 1–8. [3] Mark xvi. 9–20.

dalene, (2) to two of the disciples unnamed, (3) to the Eleven. But it is evident that this is a condensed statement from a much later date, and it is agreed by critics that this was a late addition to the Gospel. The original Mark, as preserved for us, contains, therefore, only the announcement of the resurrection to Mary Magdalene, Mary the mother of James, and Salome, by an angel, with the promise to Peter of an appearance [1] to the disciples in Galilee. This is all the more significant that the Gospel of Mark gives us no less than three predictions of His death and resurrection. [2]

The same is implied in all Jesus' predictions as to His second advent as the Son of Man on the clouds, in accordance with the conception of the Son of Man of Daniel. It seems altogether improbable, therefore, that Mark, having prepared so carefully for the event of the resurrection by these predictions, would have given no account of it in his narrative. Moreover it is evident that the Gospel without the closing section has no proper conclusion. Are

---

[1] Mark xvi. 1–8.

[2] (1) Mark viii. 31 ; Matt. xvi. 21 ; Luke ix. 22 ; (2) Mark ix. 30–32 ; Matt. xvii. 22, 23 ; Luke ix. 43–45 ; (3) Mark x. 32–34 ; Matt. xx. 17–19 ; Luke xviii. 31–34.

we to suppose that the present conclusion is a substitute for the original conclusion, owing to a mutilation of the only original manuscript, or that it has taken the place of the original conclusion by the intention of a later editor? Both of these suppositions are improbable. The Gospel of Mark has at the beginning the sentence: *"The beginning of the Gospel of Jesus Christ, the Son of God."* It is not clear whether this is a title, or the introductory clause of the sentence defined by the ministry of John the Baptist that follows. The most natural interpretation would be, if this is the title of the Gospel, that it implies a continuation of the Gospel in another and a concluding writing. The Book of Acts in the earlier chapters uses a Hebraistic source, giving an account of the origin of the Church at Jerusalem and the development of Christianity from Jerusalem as a centre to Antioch, the capital of Syria. This source is used by Luke in a similar way to his use of Mark for his Gospel. Mark, as internal evidence shows, was the most natural person to have written this narrative. He was near to St. Peter, his mother's house was the gathering place of the early Christians,[1] he was

---

[1] Acts xii. 12

present as an eye-witness of many of the remarkable scenes which are described. If he wrote the Gospel of Jesus he would also for a similar reason naturally write the story of the Jerusalem church. As he depended upon St. Peter for the one, so he depended upon St. Peter as well as himself for the other. If the Jerusalem source of Acts was a continuation of the Gospel of Jesus, we can understand better why the Gospel of Mark was the beginning of that Gospel.[1] Luke, when he distinguished between his former treatise, his Gospel, and the Book of Acts, his later treatise, simply followed his predecessor and probable source, Mark. In the opening of Acts he tells us that Jesus "*shewed himself alive after His Passion by many proofs, appearing unto them by the space of forty days, and speaking the things concerning the kingdom of God.*"[2] Two appearances after resurrection are given in the subsequent narrative: (1) one in Jerusalem to the apostles when He charged them to wait for the baptism of the Holy Spirit; (2) the other to the apostles when they asked Him respecting the restoration of the kingdom to Israel, which was at the time of the

---

[1] See p. 135.   [2] Acts i. 3.

ascension.[1] It is altogether probable that both
of these came from the Jerusalem source. Turn-
ing now to the appendix to Mark, we find the
last of these appearances condensed in Mark xvi.
19, 20, and the former in Mark xvi. 14.

Mark xvi. 12, 13, gives a condensed narrative
of the appearance of Jesus to the two disciples
at Emmaus, fully reported in Luke xxiv. 13–35.
Mark xvi. 9–11 gives an account of an appearance to Mary Magdalene. This appearance is
not given by Luke, but is given by Matthew
xxiii. 9, 10, attached to the story given by Mark
of the visit to the tomb by the Magdalene and
the other women. It is also given by John xx.
11–18, attached to the same event. On the
whole, therefore, it seems probable that though
the appendix of Mark does not come from Mark,
it yet is a condensation of the story of the resurrection, given by Mark at the beginning of his
Jerusalem source of the Book of Acts, which
was added to the Gospel by a later editor to
give it a completion, after the Gospel had been
detached from its continuation.

We would have then in the narrative of the
original Mark (1) the appearance to the Magda-

---

[1] Acts i. 4–11.

lene, (2) the appearance to the two at Emmaus,
(3) the appearance to the Eleven in Jerusalem,
(4) the appearance to the disciples at the time of
the ascension.   If so much is true, it is also
probable that the appearance to Peter, appended
to the story of the appearance to the two at
Emmaus,[1] was derived from Mark, the Petrine
source, and it is improbable that Mark would
give the message of Jesus to the disciples and
Peter, that He would appear to them in Galilee,
and not give an account of that appearance to
Peter, if he gave any appearance at all.   It is
probable also that we must add to the five appearances already mentioned, the sixth in Galilee,
reported in Matthew xxviii. 16–20.   This is
doubtless the same as the appearance of Mark
xvi. 15–18, which, however, is so condensed
that it appears as if given in connection with
the previous appearance reported by Mark in
Jerusalem.   When now we compare these six
appearances with the six given by Paul at an
earlier date, three are in both—namely (1) to
Peter, (2) to the Eleven, (3) to all the apostles.
Three are peculiar to Paul, namely (1) to the
five hundred, (2) to James, (3) to Paul.   Three

---

[1] Luke xxiv. 34.

are peculiar to Mark, (1) to the Magdalene, (2)
to the two disciples, (3) at the ascension.

We are now prepared to consider the reports
of the other Gospels, so far as they have not already been considered.   We find nothing additional in Matthew or in Luke.   They depend in
fact upon the original Mark for their narrative
here as elsewhere.   It is no more likely that we
would find additional material to any extent in
their narrative of the resurrection than in their
other narratives.   The Gospel of John, however,
gives us additional information here as elsewhere.
It enlarges upon the appearance to the Eleven,
by stating that Jesus appeared at first to ten in
the upper room, where the Lord's supper was
instituted, Thomas being absent,[1] on the day of
the resurrection ; and that in the next week He
appeared again to the Eleven, Thomas being
present.

John also reports an appearance to the seven
on the sea of Galilee,[2] thus two additional ones.
Accordingly we have ten appearances of Jesus in
all before His ascension, the one to Paul being
subsequent to the ascension.

A careful study of these appearances extending[3]

---

[1] John xx. 19–25.   [2] John xxi. 7–23.   [3] Acts i. 3.

during forty days of the fifty between Passover and Pentecost enables us to see a certain natural and appropriate progress in them. We distinguish those in Jerusalem from those in Galilee. Those in Galilee divide those in Jerusalem into two divisions, so that we really have three stages : (I.) Those in Jerusalem on the day of the resurrection and on the next Sunday. There were four appearances on the day of resurrection, (1) to Mary Magdalene, (2) to Peter, (3) to Cleopas and his companion, (4) to the Ten in the room of the Lord's Supper. (5) There was an appearance on the second Sunday to the Eleven.

(II.) Those in Galilee were : (6) to the Eleven on a mountain, (7) to the Seven by the Sea. It is probable that (8) the appearance to the five hundred reported by Paul also occurred in Galilee, and also (9) the appearance to James, the Lord's brother.

It is interesting to notice that these may be arranged on the third, fourth, fifth, and sixth Sundays after the resurrection, giving us, therefore, about a month of the forty days for the appearances in Galilee ; which indeed is altogether probable in itself. It is unlikely that the disciples would remain in Jerusalem more than a week after Passover, and so long only for good reasons. They would naturally go to their homes in Galilee, and the appearances of Jesus to the disciples there would be the ones that would confirm their faith in Him and rally them to His cause.   It is possible that there may have been other appearances not reported in the New Testament.   But it is of no slight importance that at least one of those reported may be assigned to each of the Sundays following the resurrection. These appearances of Jesus on successive Sundays may have given origin to the assembling of Christians on that day, and also to the use of the term the Lord's day.

(III.) One other appearance (10) is assigned to Jerusalem, and that at the close of the forty days, for the final interview and the ascension from the Mount of Olives.   If we suppose that forty is a round number, we have the forty-second day, the sixth Sunday, or sixth Lord's day after the resurrection, only a week before the Lord's day of Pentecost.   It is altogether probable that Jesus would choose a Lord's day for His ascension.   The disciples went up to Jerusalem the week before Pentecost, doubtless because they had been so advised by Jesus, and they were to wait in Jerusalem for the promised advent of the Spirit.   They saw Jesus ascend into heaven on

the sixth Lord's day after His resurrection.
On the seventh Lord's day the divine Spirit
came upon them as His coronation gift, endow-
ing them with the authority and energy to organ-
ize the Christian Church.

If we study these appearances of Jesus during
these forty days, we see clearly that Paul was
justified in classing the manifestation to himself
with the manifestations to the others. They
were all, indeed, revelations or manifestations—
Christophanies. Only from this point of view
can they be understood. It was indeed the same
Jesus who died and rose again, but He was not
in all respects the same. His body saw no cor-
ruption, but it did show transformation by which
it became incorruptible. The body of Jesus was
visible or invisible as He chose to make it so.
He was so different that He could not be recognized even by His intimates, unless He made
Himself known to them. His body was not
subject to the laws which govern physical substance. It was a body which might be touched
and handled, exhibiting the marks of the cross,
which might be felt as well as seen. He ate
with His disciples on one occasion. And yet
even in His first appearances in Jerusalem He
entered and left rooms without the use of en-

trances, as if He were a spirit.   And on the day
of ascension His body was not subject to the
laws of gravitation, but ascended into the air
and disappeared in the sky.   Although we may
say that He appeared to His disciples for a short
time on seven different days, yet on all other
days except these seven, and for the greater part
of these days, He was invisible, leading not an
ordinary human life, but the life of a spirit.   We
may see during these forty days indeed, a grad-
ual transformation of the earthly body into a
body prepared for the abode of spirits.

These appearances of Jesus to His disciples
were not merely to show Himself to them and
convince them that He was indeed risen, they
were also for purposes of instruction.   This is
evident from the statements of the Gospels.
They all represent that Jesus gave a final commission to the Twelve.   This is briefly stated in
varying terms in the Gospels.   But it is altogether probable, as I have shown elsewhere,[1] that
a considerable amount of the material given by
Matthew, and even Luke, in connection with the
Commission of the Twelve and the Seventy, for

---

[1] *The Apostolic Commission*, Art. i. in *Studies in Honor of B.
L. Gildersleeve.*

their missionary journeys in Galilee and Peræa, belonged really to the final commission, topical reasons alone justifying the present arrangement. The commission, as most fully given in John, is to the Seven on the sea, and especially Peter.[1] But a more limited statement is made of a commission in connection with the appearance to the Ten.[2] It is altogether probable that a part of this commission is reported out of place for topical reasons in John xv.–xvi. And the final prayer of Jesus for His disciples, John xvii., would certainly suit much better a final interview just before the Ascension, than where it now is, just before the Passion.

Luke tells us that Jesus gave His disciples full instruction respecting His fulfilment of the Messianic predictions of the Old Testament.[3] It was to be expected that He would do just this thing after His resurrection, and we can hardly explain the preaching of the Twelve as reported in the Book of Acts, based on the Jerusalem source, without some such instruction as this.

The report of the institution of the Lord's supper in the Synoptists is absent from the narrative of John. It does not altogether agree

---

[1] John xxi.   [2] John xx. 19–23.   [3] Luke xxiv. 44–46.

with the report of Paul.   We could not prove
from the Synoptists that it was anything more
than the institution of the new Covenant, ob-
served once for all.   But Paul tells us that it
was instituted as a permanent institution until
the second advent of the Lord, and that it represented not only a new Covenant, but that it
stands for the Christian annual Passover, and
also for all the thank-offerings and peace-offer-
ings of the old dispensation, involving frequent
observance.[1]

The narratives of the Book of Acts, based on
the Jerusalem source, report the observance of
the Lord's supper as a habit of the Christians
from the beginning.[2]   When now we turn to
the Gospel of John,[3] we find a specific command
to eat the flesh and drink the blood of Christ as
a condition of everlasting life.   This can be understood with difficulty in its present context.
It clearly refers to the Holy Eucharist, but it is
given here out of place, before its institution, because of its parallelism in topic with the bread
from heaven, about which Jesus has been dis-
coursing.   It is probable that these words have

---

[1] 1 Cor. v. 7, x. 16–21, xi. 23–26.   See *Messiah of the Apostles,* pp. 100 *seq.*

[2] Acts ii. 42, xx. 7–11.   [3] John vi. 51–57.

been taken from a post-resurrection discourse of Jesus; that this is just the discourse upon which the perpetual observance of the Lord's Supper depends; that Paul has combined in his narrative the discourse on the night of the betrayal with this post-resurrection discourse; and that the observance of the Lord's Supper of the early Christians depends upon this combined teaching.[1] There must have been similar teaching of Jesus as to Baptism, for there is a mysterious gap between the Baptism of the Gospels and the Baptism of the Apostolic History. It is true the command to baptize is in the apostolic commission, but there are many questions which must have arisen, which seem to have occasioned no difficulty in the practice of the Apostolic Church. The commission of the Twelve is evident enough in the Gospels; but what shall we say of the Seventy? They doubtless are at the basis of the larger group of disciples, one hundred and twenty in number, who appear in Jerusalem, waiting for the advent of the Spirit, from whom the successor of Judas was chosen,[2] and who, equally with the Twelve, received the endowment of the

---

[1] See *Messiah of the Gospels,* pp. 122 *seq.*
[2] Acts i. 21–26.

divine Spirit.   They reappear doubtless in the
prophets of the Apostolic Church, of whom Barnabas was the most eminent.   How far they
shared the commission given to the Twelve, the
Gospels do not inform us.   The appearance to
the five hundred, reported by Paul, could hardly
have been without some instruction on the part
of Jesus.   We are justified, therefore, in the conclusion that we must assign no inconsiderable
portion of the teaching of Jesus to His appearances after His resurrection.   It is upon the ex-
periences of these forty days, as much as upon
the year and a half of the previous ministry of
Jesus, that the faith and life of the Apostolic
Church was grounded.

XI

THE SYNOPTIC PROBLEM

THE three Gospels, Matthew, Mark, and Luke, are named the Synoptic Gospels. They have so much material that is common, and this material is in great measure so alike in substance and form, that it is impossible to explain it on the basis of independent oral sources. Written sources certainly lie at the basis of a large part of the material that is common to them.

It is agreed by the vast majority of recent critics, and it may be regarded as a sure result of criticism, that these three Gospels depend upon the Logia of St. Matthew, composed, as Papias tells us, in the Hebrew language. It is also agreed that Mark is the earliest of the three Synoptic Gospels, and that Matthew and Luke use the original Mark as well as the Logia of St. Matthew as their source. When now we come to consider the Logia of St. Matthew there are several problems that have not yet been solved by common consent.

1. Notwithstanding Eusebius reports[1] that Papias represented that the Logia was written in the Hebrew language, a large number of scholars insist that by Hebrew he meant Aramaic, the language spoken by the Jews of Palestine in the time of our Lord. The most prominent advocate of this opinion in recent times is Dalman.[2] I myself held that opinion for many years before Dalman discussed the subject. But, as I said in 1897,[3] "A special study of all the supposed material of the Logia has since convinced me that the original was Hebrew." Resch[4] has since given abundant evidence for this opinion, in his discussion of the subject and his attempt to give the Logia in the original Hebrew. The arguments of Dalman, in favor of an Aramaic original, seem quite strong, especially to those who have not made an independent study of the question; but they amount to no more than an Aramaic original of some words of Jesus and His disciples. All admit that Jesus and His dis-

---

[1] *Church History*, III., xxiv. 6 ; xxxix. 16. Trans. McGiffert, pp. 152, 173.

[2] Dalman, *Die Worte Jesus*, 1898 ; cf. Meyer, *Jesu Muttersprache*, 1896.

[3] *Expository Times*, June, 1897.

[4] Resch, *Die Logia Jesu*, 1898.

ciples used the Aramaic in their speech. This is not the question; but it is whether the written Logia was in Aramaic or Hebrew. The evidences for an Aramaic original given by Dalman prove no more than Aramaic original speech. But the arguments for a Hebrew original, so far as they are valid, prove a written Hebrew original, for all admit that Hebrew was not the speech of our Lord.

In fact, it is altogether improbable that Matthew would have written his Gospel in Aramaic. Aramaic was the language of speech and not the language of literature. No literature of any importance in the Aramaic language is known from the times of our Lord. The literary language of all educated Jews in Palestine and the East at that time was Hebrew. Anyone who could read, could read Hebrew. Hebrew was not only the sacred language of the Old Testament Scriptures, but also of all the Apocrypha and Pseudepigrapha, except of the few written in Greek for the Hellenistic Jews. The sayings of the Jewish Fathers of the times of Jesus, and subsequently, are in Hebrew. The Mishnayoth and the Baraithoth, the earliest elements of the Talmud, and the earliest Commentaries on the Old Testament among the Jews, were written in Hebrew.   Indeed it was not until many generations after the death of Jesus that Aramaic became the literary language of the Jews.   Therefore there was no motive for composing a Gospel in Aramaic, and every motive for composing it in Hebrew.   The Aramaic was a language of common speech, but of many dialects, and there were no great writings of universal importance, and no common literature to give a common standard for the language throughout the Aramaic-speaking world.   The language of Galilee was rude to the Jerusalemite, that of Palestine difficult to understand by the Jews of Babylon.   But the Hebrew language was the common sacred language of the Jewish world, and anyone who wished to write a religious book, and especially one that would be of an authoritative character, was compelled by the situation to write it in Hebrew.   We should have no doubt therefore that the original language of Matthew's Logia was Hebrew.

2. Another problem of still greater difficulty remains unsolved.   Resch follows Weiss and earlier scholars generally in the opinion that the Logia of Matthew gave not only words of Jesus, but also historical incidents.

Here I must differ from him.   The Logia, as

I have attempted to show,[1] was composed entirely of the Wisdom of Jesus—that is sayings
in the gnomic poetic form, of the type known
in the Proverbs, Job, and Ecclesiastes of the
Old Testament, the Wisdom of Sirach and Wisdom of Solomon of the Apocrypha, and the
sayings of the Fathers in the Mishna.[2] These
sayings of Wisdom represent a method of teaching used by the Rabbis of the time of Jesus,
which Jesus used and in which He excelled all.
These logia, or sayings of Wisdom, are given
by the present Gospel of Matthew in several
great collections. The chief of these is the so-
called Sermon on the Mount.[3] The other collections are the Commission of the Twelve, and
sayings on their return from their Mission,[4] and
the Woes against the Pharisees.[5] Luke gives
this material scattered throughout his Gospel,
attached frequently to historical incidents, some
of which are similar to those of Mark. The
weight of evidence, therefore, is in favor of these
having been spoken on a great number of occa-

---

[1] Articles upon the Wisdom of Jesus in the *Expository Times*
in 1897.

[2] *General Introduction to the Study of Holy Scripture*, pp.
385 *seq*.

[3] Matt. v.–vii.   [4] Matt. x., xi.   [5] Matt. xxiii.

sions as a characteristic of Jesus' teaching, and
not in three or four great discourses, as Matthew
arranges them; and that, therefore, the grouping
of them in Matthew's Gospel is due to the author of that Gospel and not to his source, the
Logia of Matthew.   This is confirmed by the recently discovered collection of Logia of Jesus,[1] in
which each one is introduced by "*Jesus says:*"—
This peculiarity is preserved frequently in Mark,
but not in Matthew.   On the whole, therefore,
we may conclude that Luke gives us the logia
more in accordance with their order and form in
the Logia of Matthew, although even Luke does
not hesitate to group them for topical reasons.
We have already seen[2] that in all probability
Matthew and Thomas were the apostolic pair
that accompanied Jesus in the Peræan ministry.
It is altogether probable, therefore, that Matthew
in his Logia gave the Peræan logia together and
the Galilean logia together.   It is improbable
that he gave them all in connection with the
Galilean ministry, or in connection with the
Woes on the Pharisees in Passion Week, where
the present Gospel of Matthew gives them.   At

---

[1] Λογια Ιησου, *Sayings of our Lord,* from an Early Greek
Papyrus, discovered and edited by Grenfell and Hunt, 1897.

[2] See p. 76.

the same time it is unlikely that many of them had any more than a brief statement of the occasion; and it is probable that in many cases they were simply introduced by the words—"*Jesus said*"—when it was deemed unimportant to mention the incident out of which they sprang. Unless this be so, it is difficult to understand, and indeed impossible to explain, how the author of the present Gospel of Matthew threw away such a large number of historical incidents and utterly disregarded them, when he gave these logia in the several great collections. And this is all the more inexplicable that his Gospel bears the name of Matthew, because it was supposed Matthew's Logia was its essential substance. This argument is still more insuperable if, with Weiss, Resch, and most scholars, we suppose that the Logia comprised so great a portion of the historical material given in Matthew and Mark. How then can we explain on the one hand the drastic way in which Luke attaches so great a portion of the logia to incidents of the Peræan ministry, and on the other hand, the no less drastic way in which the author of Matthew's Gospel takes the logia out of their historical connection and gives them in several great groups? If we suppose that the Logia of Matthew con-

tained so large an amount of historical material
as Resch gives in his reconstruction, all coming
from Matthew, an eye-witness, it is difficult to
see how Luke, the best historian of the New
Testament, could have taken such liberties with
a source of so great authority. It is also difficult to find a sufficient amount of original material in Mark, not derived from the supposed
Logia, to justify the tradition, even more
strongly supported than the authorship of the
Logia of Matthew, that Mark depended upon
St. Peter for his source. The historical material given in the Logia of Resch is not very much
less than what we are obliged to find in the
original Mark. The conclusion which seems on
the whole most probable is that the Logia contained only the Wisdom of Jesus arranged very
much in the order in which the logia appear in
Luke, with occasional brief statements of the
occasion on which they were uttered.

The historical material of the three Synoptists
was derived from the original Mark. The general opinion among modern critics is that the
original Mark differed but slightly from the
canonical Mark. All admit certain additions,
the chief of which is the Appendix.[1] Other ad-

---

[1] Mark xvi. 9 *seq*.

ditions here and there must be recognized. Unless the whole of the eschatological discourse [1] be an addition, we must certainly suppose that of the several duplicates contained there, one of each is an addition. If the story of the feeding of the five thousand [2] is only a variation of the feeding of the four thousand, [3] one of them is an addition to the Gospel. It is probable that the logia respecting the sin against the Holy Spirit and of Beelzebub, [4] attached by Matthew and Luke [5] to an appropriate historical incident, is not only attached by Mark to the wrong incident, and at too early a date, against the usage of Mark, but is an addition to Mark by a second hand. [6] There are several other groups of logia that are not in harmony with their context, and seem to come from a second hand. Other important additions may be detected in other places in the Gospel. And so it seems improbable that the original Mark used the Logia of Matthew. When these additions have all been stripped off,

---

[1] Mark xiii.   [2] Mark vi. 34 *seq.*

[3] Mark viii. 1 *seq.*   [4] Mark iii. 22–30.

[5] Matt. xii. 22 *seq.;* Luke xi. 14 *seq.*

[6] I have made a special study of all the logia used in Mark, which I hope soon to publish. The opinion given above is the result of that study.

there remains a Gospel of considerable bulk, giving few discourses of Jesus, but a general outline
of His brief ministry. Internal evidence confirms
the ancient tradition that the preaching of Peter
underlies this Gospel.   It knows only of a Galilean ministry and Passion week in Jerusalem.
It knows nothing of the ministry in Peræa of
Luke, or of the Jerusalem ministry of John.
The reason was that St. Peter confined his testimony to what he himself had seen and heard.
He was not with Jesus during the Jerusalem or
the Peræan ministries, and therefore these do not
appear in his Gospel.

The present Mark was prepared for Gentile
Christians in the Greek language. The question
now arises as to the language of the original
Mark.   It is the general opinion that St. Mark
wrote in Greek.   But St. Peter and St. Mark
were both Jews. Hebrew was the language
that they would use, if the Gospel was written
originally for Jewish Christians, even if these
were in Rome.   I agree, therefore, with Resch
that the greater part of the historical material at
the basis of the Synoptists came from a Hebrew
source.   I disagree with him in that he thinks of
one source, St. Matthew, whereas I think of
two,—the Logia of St. Matthew for the Wisdom

of Jesus, and the Petrine Mark for the Galilean
ministry and Passion week. These were the
two written sources of the Synoptists. The
Greek Mark is a translation of the original Mark
with an occasional use of the Logia of Matthew,
and other additions.

It is also my opinion, which I share with
Blass,[1] that Mark was the author of the Jerusalem source of the Book of Acts, written also in
the Hebrew language, based also on Peter's
preaching; and that this was a second part, or
continuation of the Gospel of Mark.[2]

The Greek Gospel of Matthew uses the original
Mark as the framework for the history, and therefore limits itself to the Galilean ministry and Passion week. But it uses also the Logia of St.
Matthew and arranges the material in great collections on the framework of the narrative of Mark.
The parables of Matthew are additional to Mark.
Some of them are given by Luke in connection
with the Peræan ministry and derived from oral
tradition, as their different versions clearly show.
Matthew also groups these parables about the

---

[1] Blass, *Acta Apost.* 1896, s. iv. *seq.; Philology of the Gospels,*
1898, pp. 141 *seq.* See also the earlier query of Weiss, *Marcus
evangelium*, 1872, s. 511.

[2] See pp. 112 *seq.*

kindred parables of Mark, making chiefly four
collections: (1) The parables of the Kingdom,
(2) The parables of Instruction of the Disciples
on His last journey to Jerusalem, (3) the parables attached to the conflict with the Pharisees
in Passion week, and (4) the parables attached
to the eschatological discourse.[1]   Matthew also
gives a brief gospel of the infancy of Jesus,
which we reserve for special consideration.

The Gospel of Luke uses the same two sources
as Matthew, only he adds to them material derived from other sources oral and written.   In
the main he follows the order of Mark in the
first part of his Gospel, and gives his additional
material in the second part of his Gospel, before
the final crisis in Passion week.   This additional
material, while it is composed of several important events, doubtless of the Peræan ministry,
derived probably from an oral source, is chiefly
composed of parables and logia.   In his use of
the Logia in the first part of his work, he undoubtedly gives us the correct version of the
Sermon on the Mount, and the Commission of
the Twelve ; and so in all probability the proper
historical connection of the most of the other

---

[1] See p. 74.

logia. We may therefore conclude that the logia assigned by him to the Peræan ministry also for the most part belong there ; and that in this he follows the Logia of Matthew, only that in the Logia of Matthew, the logia given by Luke in the Peræan ministry, detached from those which he gives in the Galilean ministry, were not so clearly attached to a Peræan ministry and historical incidents, that the author of Matthew's Gospel was debarred from using them in another connection. The most of the parables given by Luke in this section of his gospel are of a very different character from those given in Mark and Matthew. They are parables of grace and salvation. They were doubtless derived from an oral source, and are most appropriate in the Peræan ministry. I see no reason to follow Weiss and think of a written source other than the two already given, for this section of Luke. The incidents are too few to justify such a conclusion.

Luke gives, in his earlier chapters, an extended gospel of the infancy of Jesus, which he must have derived from other sources of information than those already considered. This we must reserve for special consideration.

And so the three Synoptic Gospels gradually

came into existence. The Logia of Matthew and the Gospel of St. Mark were the fundamental Gospels written in the Hebrew language, having apostolic origin from eye- and ear-witnesses of the ministry of Jesus. The composition of the other Gospels was due in part to the needs of the Gentile world, and so these original Gospels were translated with explanations. There was also an increasing demand for more information as to the life and teaching of Jesus, which could be satisfied only by searching out other eye-witnesses and ear-witnesses, who could testify as to the things they had seen and heard and knew. The author of Matthew's Gospel did but little of this ; but Luke, as he himself tells us, was zealous and painstaking ; and his Gospel, when compared with the others, amply justifies and attests his own statements. St. Luke wrote last of the three. His work was certainly unknown to the author of Matthew's Gospel. He wrote his Gospel before he wrote the Book of Acts. He was the physician and pupil of St. Paul. But he was not his companion on his travels as tradition has wrongly inferred. According to the New Testament he first appears in connection with St. Paul at the close of his life in Rome,[1]

---

[1] Col. iv. 14.

and therefore was a younger man than tradition allows. His Gospel was written subsequent to the death of the great apostle; subsequent also, as internal evidence shows, to the destruction of Jerusalem by the Romans, probably in the eighties of the first century. Many of the first disciples of Jesus had died, but many others were still living—and, indeed, a sufficient number to secure testimony of the first historical importance. Without the Gospel of Luke a serious loss would be felt in our knowledge of the ministry of Jesus.

XII

THE COMPOSITION OF THE GOSPEL OF JOHN

TWO antagonistic views have been battling for a century with regard to the composition of the Gospel of John. The traditional view maintains the authorship of St. John the apostle. The view held by most critics is that it was the work of a pupil of St. John. Many strong, and indeed insuperable arguments are adduced in favor of the authorship of St. John. Equally numerous, strong, and insuperable arguments are adduced against his authorship. Those who take either side of the controversy depreciate and endeavor to explain away and avoid the arguments of the other side, but without success. Neither view has been able to overcome the other. The reason, as ought by this time to be obvious, is that neither view is correct. The problem cannot be solved by either side of this debate. Under these circumstances it is remarkable that another method was not earlier used ; especially as the method of analysis has solved so many problems in the Old Testament ; and all the more that the problems of the Gospels of Matthew and Luke have been solved in this way; and those of the Book of Acts are in process of solution. The Book of Revelations has also been analyzed into several documents.[1] Several of the Epistles, such as II. Corinthians and the Pastorals, have been explained in this way, and even the closing chapter of Romans must be detached from that epistle and given an independent value.[2]

The reason why this method has not been used to solve the problem of the Fourth Gospel is doubtless the striking unity of that Gospel. This unity, which is so evident, is indeed an obstruction to the method of analysis; but it is not an insuperable one. The New Testament writers use their sources in a different way from the Old Testament writers. It is much easier to analyze Old Testament books than New Testament books for the reason that the Old Testament writers preserve the very language of their sources, and piece these together by seams of their own composition. The New Testament

---

[1] *Messiah of the Apostles*, pp. 284 *seq.*
[2] *General Introduction*, p. 315.

writers, however, use their sources more freely, condensing, enlarging, and explaining, and not unfrequently rewriting, so as to change the language and style of their originals.

We have also to consider, in many cases, the process of translation from the Hebrew into the Greek language. This is evident in the use of the poetical logia by Matthew and Luke. It is still more the case in the use of the original narratives of Mark by Matthew and Luke. Luke is much freer in his use of the original Mark than Matthew, and he pursues the same method in his use of the Jerusalem source of the Book of Acts.

The Book of Acts has indeed as striking a unity as the Fourth Gospel. This has made the work of analysis more difficult, and has retarded it, so that the problem has not yet been fully solved; but it has not prevented critics from using this method. Why, then, should the unity of the Gospel of John obstruct the analysis of that Gospel? No serious attempt to analyze the Fourth Gospel was made until recent years, when Wendt undertook it.[1]

---

[1] Wendt, *Das Johannesevangelium*, 1900. Independent of Wendt, and prior to the publication of his views, I had tried the same method, and I had come to the conclusion that this

The very fact that there are such strong and convincing arguments both for and against the authorship of the Fourth Gospel by St. John, raises the question whether the arguments for his authorship, so far as they are derived from the Gospel itself, may not belong to one strata of the Gospel, and the arguments against his authorship to another strata? This is indeed the true state of the case. When now we apply the principles and method of the Higher Criticism to the analysis of this Gospel, we find that there are linguistic and stylistic differences, differences of historical situation, differences of opinion and conception, and the arguments from citation and from silence are not without forceful representation. I cannot, in the space allotted to me in the proportions of this volume, undertake a full proof of this statement. I shall only give a few specimens of evidence.

(1) There is a striking difference in the Gos-

---

was the only method by which we could solve the problem of the Fourth Gospel. I published my view without argument in the first edition of my *General Introduction to the Study of Holy Scripture*, 1899, p. 327. In essentials, I agree in my analysis with Wendt. We differ less than the earlier analysts of the Hexateuch, notwithstanding the greater difficulty of the analysis.

pel in the use of σημεῖα, signs for miracles,[1] and the use of ἔργα, works.[2] All the uses of σημεῖα are in sections which are clearly from the final author, or may be from him. The only instances that may be disputed are, Chapter iii. 2, in the words of Nicodemus, and Chapters iv. 48, vi. 26, in the words of Jesus, both of which are rebukes of the people for sign-seeking. Jesus Himself always uses ἔργα when speaking of His own miracles. This is indeed in accordance with the usage of the New Testament elsewhere. The original Mark and the Logia always use δυνάμεις for miracles; σημεῖα belongs to the later strata, especially of Luke. There is, indeed, in these strata not only a difference of terms, but also an earlier and a later conception of the nature and meaning of miracles.

(2) A difference of historical situation is involved in the use, for the opponents of Jesus in Jerusalem, of the terms *Pharisees* and *Jews*. The Synoptic Gospels use *Pharisees* for the chief opponents of Jesus. So the use of *Pharisees* in the Fourth Gospel belongs to the original strata,

---

[1] John ii. 11, 18, 23, iii. 2, iv. 48, 54, vi. 2, 14, 26, 30, vii. 31, ix. 16, x. 41, xi. 47, xii. 18, 37, xx. 30.

[2] John v. 20, 36, vii. 3, 21, ix. 3, 4, x. 25, 32, 33, 37, 38, xiv. 10, 11, 12, xv. 24.

but the common use of Jews for the enemies belongs to a later strata, and indeed indicates a historical situation, when the distinction between Jew and Christian had been so sharpened that the Jew, as such, was hostile to Christ and Christianity. The apostle St. John could never have so written about his countrymen—he, least of all the apostles, because of his intimate association with families in Jerusalem.

(3) A difference of doctrinal conception is recognized by most scholars in the dogmatic elaboration of the discourse of Jesus to Nicodemus,[1] and of the Baptist.[2] But such dogmatic expositions of conversations of Jesus are characteristic of the Gospel and appear in most of the sections. Thus in John v. 28, 29, we have a distinct prediction of a universal resurrection, which is attached to another and entirely different conception of resurrection. In the Synoptists there is no reference to a resurrection of the wicked. Without these verses the Fourth Gospel agrees with the Synoptists. With them, it agrees with the latest strata of the New Testament. There can be little doubt that this is a dogmatic addi-

---

[1] John iii. 16–21. See *Messiah of the Apostles,* pp. 515 *seq.*
[2] John iii. 31–36.

tion to the original Gospel.   The situation at this
feast was not so grave as this writer represents.
Jesus had not yet asserted His divinity as this
author thinks, when he says, " *For this cause
therefore the Jews sought the more to kill him,
because he not only brake the Sabbath, but also
called God his own Father, making himself equal
with God.*" [1]

A considerable amount of the work of the
author of the present Gospel may easily be
detected and removed.   But after that has been
done we cannot say that he has left the Gospel
in its original form.   He has indeed rewritten
the original, even to a greater extent than Luke
rewrote his sources.   This is evident in the use
of the few logia preserved in the Fourth Gospel,
where the words and expressions are sometimes
entirely different from those of the Synoptists,
and the gnomic form has disappeared. [2]   The
same is true of the conversations of Jesus and
His longer discourses, and even with the historical incidents.   At the same time, even
here, careful criticism may distinguish the final
author's handiwork, and detect the original Gospel which underlies it.   This rewriting of the

---

[1] John v. 18.   [2] See *General Introduction*, pp. 69–70.

original was probably due to the fact that the original Gospel was in the Hebrew language, and it had become necessary to translate it into Greek. Matthew and Luke use the Logia of St. Matthew, and the original Mark, in a similar way. All three of the primitive Gospels were written by Hebrews in the Hebrew language, with which they were familiar, and for the use of Jewish Christians. In fact the Gospel of John, especially in those parts which belong to the earliest strata, is in some respects the most Hebraistic of the Gospels. In none of them are there so many explanations of Hebrew and Aramaic words and phrases.

If then we may distinguish an original Gospel of John underlying the Fourth Gospel, very much as we distinguished a Gospel of Matthew underlying the first Gospel, the several remaining problems become easier of solution. It is evident that the original Gospel closed with:[1] "*Many other signs therefore did Jesus in the presence of the disciples, which are not written in this book: but these are written, that ye may believe that Jesus is the Christ, the Son of God; and that believing ye may have life in his name.*"

---

[1] John xx. 30–31.

Chapter xxi., as is generally agreed, was a subsequent addition, and, as we may now say, by
a third hand; for the concluding verses[1] evidently came not from the apostle St. John but
from the second hand; as it uses the term
σημεῖα, expressing clearly the dogmatic intent
of the author, and the chief aim of the book, not
only to show that Jesus is the Messiah, the Son
of God, but that life is through faith in Him.

The Prologue, as I have shown elsewhere,[2] is
a hymn to the Logos, composed independently
of the Gospel, and prefixed to it. In the present
Gospel it is interwoven with the introduction to
the story of the Baptist, destroying in part its
metrical form. It is probable that it was not
attached to the original Gospel, but was prefixed by the second hand, and interwoven by the
third hand.

When now we turn to the Gospel as left by
the second hand, with the hymn to the Logos
prefixed, it begins, as Mark does, with a brief
account of the preparatory ministry of the Baptist, and concludes with the appearance of Jesus,
after the resurrection, to the Eleven in Jerusalem.

---

[1] John xx. 30–31.
[2] See *Messiah of the Apostles*, pp. 495–515.

We have in our previous studies seen abundant evidence that the material is not arranged in chronological order in the present Gospel.[1] It is important that we should briefly restate the case, and consider whether the present order is due to the original author or to the second hand.

The story of the naming of St. Peter is attached to the first meeting of Jesus with Andrew, his brother, before the first Galilean ministry,[2] when it properly belongs, according to the Synoptists, at the close of the Galilean ministry, in connection with the Confession at Cæsarea Philippi.[3] The conversation with Nathanael, with its distinct statement and recognition of the Messiahship of Jesus,[4] is undoubtedly also too early to be harmonized with the attitude of the disciples during the early part of Jesus' ministry, according to the Synoptists. The Fourth Gospel aims to prove the Messiahship of Jesus, at the very beginning of the Gospel, and it places the calling of disciples, all that are mentioned, in one place at the beginning, doubtless for topical reasons. If this order was in the original Gospel of John, we must recog-

---

[1] See pp. 10, 45, 47, 50 *seq.*
[2] John i. 40–42.
[3] See *General Introduction,* pp. 514 *seq.*
[4] John i. 49.

nize that St. John had the same motive as his pupil, who revised and edited his work. But this is improbable, for there is an implicit inconsistency between the assured faith of these disciples prior to the ministry, and their expression of that faith after testing.[1] The latter is more in accord with the Synoptists, and intrinsically more probable.

The cleansing of the temple is given[2] at a Passover usually regarded as the first of Jesus' ministry. The same event is given by the Synoptists at the last Passover. It is improbable that this event occurred twice. Jesus would not have been so imprudent as to force an issue, and so sharp and perilous an issue, at so early a date in His ministry. Furthermore the implicit reference to His death and resurrection[3] is too early to be reconciled with Synoptic statements. And the reflection of the author[4] that many believed Him because they had seen the σημεῖα, that He wrought, is out of place at so early a date, when the only sign thus far wrought, according even to the Gospel of John, was at Cana of Galilee, at a marriage feast whose only witnesses were the guests of the occasion.

---

[1] John vi. 66–69.

[2] John ii. 13–25.

[3] John ii. 19–22.

[4] John ii. 23.

The report of the Fourth Gospel itself, therefore, is inconsistent with this early placing of the
event. The motive, again, is to give a distinct
and public assertion of His Messiahship, as accepted by many in Jerusalem, near the beginning
of the Gospel, immediately after the showing
forth of His power at Cana of Galilee.

The conversation with Nicodemus,[1] even after
it has been stripped of its later dogmatic additions, is still out of place. It doubtless is not in
chronological order. It could not be earlier than
the reference to Nicodemus at the feast of Tabernacles.[2] It is placed by Tatian much later.
The motive for the present placing of the story is
to set forth the impression made by Jesus upon
a member of the Sanhedrim.

The story of the journey through Samaria and
the proclaiming of His Messiahship by Jesus,
and the faith of the Samaritans in Him,[3] is certainly too early—too early for such an assertion
of His Messiahship, and too early for a journey
through Samaria northward, which implies a

---

[1] John iii. 1–21.

[2] John vii. 50–52. The statement in parentheses, " *he that
came to him before, being one of them,*" verse 50, is from the
second or third hand.

[3] John iv. 4–42.

peril which did not exist until after the resurrection of Lazarus.[1] The motive for its present place in the Gospel is to set forth the acceptance of Jesus as the Messiah by the Samaritans.

The story of the healing of the nobleman's son[2] was probably not in the original John, because its difference from the corresponding event described in the Synoptic Gospels is so great that it indicates not only different oral tradition, but also a form of statement which could hardly have come from St. John the apostle, who was familiar with Capernaum, and was an eye-witness of the event, according to the Synoptists.

Thus far the Fourth Gospel has set forth the acceptance of Jesus as Messiah by the Baptist, by several disciples, by Nicodemus, a member of the Sanhedrim, by Galileans, Judæans, and Samaritans. The author now tells of a series of conflicts with the unbelievers. The story begins in Jerusalem, Chapter v., then is transferred to Galilee, Chapter vi., only to return to Jerusalem from Chapter vii. until the end.

Chapter v. begins with a reference to an indefinite feast.[3] All the other feasts are definite, why not this? It is improbable that St. John,

---

[1] See pp. 91 *seq.*   [2] John iv. 46–54.   [3] See p. 51.

from whom the statements as to the other feasts came, did not know what this feast was. We can only think that the author of the present Gospel took this incident from a connection, in which the feast was defined, and gave it a position in his narrative apart from its historical introduction. Otherwise the statement as to the feast came from a supposition of the author, without being in his original. At all events, Chapter vi. is out of place chronologically. It should come after Chapter xi. Its present position is topical, to give the Galilean rejection before devoting attention to the great struggle in Jerusalem. It is improbable that this was the order of the original John.

Chapters vii.–x. give a series of controversial dialogues between Jesus and the Pharisees in Jerusalem, separated by accounts of two journeys to Jerusalem, one to Tabernacles, one to Dedication; and supplemented, Chapter xi., by a third journey to the raising of Lazarus. These three events are doubtless in the order given. But it does not by any means follow that all of the material of these chapters was originally in the order in which it now appears. Chapter vii. 37–52 gives a discourse on the last and great day of the feast of Tabernacles, followed by a delibera-

tion of the Sanhedrim respecting Jesus. It is
rather remarkable that this is followed by Chapter viii.–x. 21, before the material connected with
the feast of Dedication. The feast of Tabernacles having closed, it was natural that Jesus
should depart with the multitudes from Jerusalem, and there is reason to think that the first
Peræan ministry immediately followed that feast.[1]
It is also improbable that Jesus would have remained in Jerusalem after the crisis reported at
the close of Chapter viii.

Moreover, the material of these chapters seems
at too early a date for the development of the
conflict with the Pharisees.[2] This material is
better suited to the situation at the feast of
Dedication than to the situation at the feast of
Tabernacles several months before.

In the present text Chapter viii. begins with
the story of the woman taken in adultery,[3] when
Jesus enters into the temple from the Mount of
Olives, just as He did in Passion week daily,
according to the Synoptists. It is agreed by all
critics that this is a late addition to the Gospel—
later indeed than the additions of the third hand.
But the very fact, that it was inserted here in

---

[1] See p. 67.   [2] See pp. 83 *seq*.   [3] John viii. 1–11.

some early manuscript, makes it evident that a gap in the Gospel was detected just at this point.

The distinct reference to His death [1] implies greater peril than any yet experienced, and is more suited to the peril of the feast of Dedication. The denunciation of His opponents,[2] the statement of His pre-existence,[3] and the attempt of the people to stone Him for blasphemy [4] also seem better suited to that occasion when He was doomed, and had no longer any reason for reserve or caution. The story of healing the man born blind, Chapter ix., and its consequences, is also more suited to the latter date. Chapter x. 1–21, the allegory of the Good Shepherd, is indeed implied in x. 26–29, and probably originally preceded it. The attempt at stoning, x. 31, seems to be the same as that of viii. 59. The separation of this material was doubtless due to the second author, as more suited to his dogmatic reflections, and it can hardly be ascribed to the original Gospel of John.

Chapters xiii.–xvii. give a connected series of discourses of Jesus with His disciples on Passion eve. But there is a break at the close of Chap-

---

[1] John viii. 12–29.

[2] John viii. 30–50.

[3] John viii. 51–58.

[4] John viii. 59.

ter xiv., where Jesus is represented as saying: " *Arise, let us go hence.*" It is remarkable that discourses with the disciples continue through Chapters xv., xvi., concluding with a final prayer of Jesus for His disciples, Chapter xvii. When these discourses are examined critically it is evident that we have a complexity of material not altogether suited to the situation on the eve of the Passion. The dogmatic intent of the author is evident in his additions to the discussions of Jesus and His disciples.

Chapter xvii. and a considerable amount of material in the previous chapters suit much better a post-resurrection situation in connection with the final commission of the disciples ; and the prayer is best suited to the last interview with the disciples just prior to the ascension, as reported in Luke.[1]

It is evident, therefore, that the discourses of Jesus and the few historical incidents in the Fourth Gospel are arranged with a dogmatic purpose and in a topical order. Nothing can be more unsafe than to treat them as in chronological order. The arrangement of modern harmonists and authors of the life of Jesus, which is

---

[1] See p. 121.

based upon this theory of the chronological order of the Fourth Gospel, is, therefore, altogether wrong. It obstructs the way to an understanding of the development in the life of Jesus, and fills the whole story with darkness and confusion. It is not surprising that many moderns disregard the Fourth Gospel altogether in their studies of the life of Jesus.

If, however, we abandon this error, use the material of the Fourth Gospel, after the example of the earliest harmonist, Tatian, as in topical order, and then seek to arrange it where it best fits into the narratives of the Synoptists; or if we use all the material of the Fourth Gospel, without prejudice as to its chronological order, with the other Gospels as common sources for an arrangement of the material as it best suits all the conditions of the problem, a new light breaks forth upon the whole, and the material falls naturally into an orderly development and a harmonious historical narrative.

If the results thus far obtained are correct, not the apostle St. John, but his pupil is responsible for the structure of the Fourth Gospel. He uses the original Hebrew Gospel of St. John as his source, just as the author of the Gospel of Matthew uses the original Gospel of St.

Matthew as his source; but the order of the discourses of Jesus in the original Gospel of St. John is even more clouded than the order of the logia in the original Gospel of St. Matthew. Their historical order we may determine partly from incidental statements contained therein; but chiefly from the interrelation of their teachings and their appropriate fitting into the events of the life of Jesus after these have taken their place in the narrative.

XIII

THE GOSPEL OF THE INFANCY

THE Gospels of Mark and John agree in having no gospel of the Infancy of Jesus. This was due doubtless to a lack of interest in that part of the life of Jesus, as well as to the fact that both of these Gospels seem to be limited to the testimony of what the primary authorities themselves had seen and heard—St. Peter in Mark, and St. John in the Gospel of John—that is, in both Gospels in their original forms.

The later editors, doubtless owing to a more dogmatic interest, thinking of Jesus as the Son of God and divine, had still less interest in the infancy of Jesus. The Gospel of the Infancy is confined to a brief statement in Matthew i. 18–ii. to which a genealogy of Jesus is prefixed; and a fuller statement, Luke i.–ii. to which a genealogy is appended, iii. 23–38, the ministry of John being inserted, iii. 1–22.

The fact, that in both cases the gospel of the

Infancy is attached to genealogies shows an interest in proving that Jesus was the Son of David, the heir of the promises to David and his seed, and so the Messiah. The fact that Luke's genealogy goes back to Adam shows a human interest, and a universalism characteristic of the Roman disciple of St. Paul. The stories of the Infancy, told by Matthew, were all to show that Jesus was the Messiah of Prophecy:[1] (1) The annunciation to Joseph and birth of Jesus, as the fulfilment of the prophecy of Isaiah respecting Emmanuel ;[2] (2) The adoration of the Magi, as the fulfilment of the prophecy of Micah that the Messiah would be born in Bethlehem ;[3] (3) The blood-bath of Bethlehem and flight into Egypt, as fulfilling the prophecy of Jeremiah, of Rachel weeping for her children ; and the prediction of Hosea that—"*out of Egypt did I call my son ;*"[4] (4) The return to Nazareth, as fulfilling the prophecy of Isaiah[5] that He should be called a Nazarene.

It is evident that none of this was found in the original Gospels of Matthew or Mark. These

---

[1] *Messiah of the Gospels,* pp. 318 *seq.*

[2] Matt. i. 18–25 ; Is. vii. 14.   [3] Matt. ii. 1–12 ; Mic. v. 2.

[4] Matt. ii. 13–18 ; Jer. xxxi. 15 ; Hos. xi. 1.

[5] Matt. ii. 19–23 ; Is. xi. 1.

are all additions inserted by the author of the canonical Matthew. This conception of the fulfilment of Old Testament prophecy by these events as stated by this author, is doubtless a crude interpretation of the Old Testament Scripture.[1] We may, however, find a sufficient number of parallels in the Rabbinical methods of the time. We are to explain them, therefore, not in accordance with modern principles of interpretation, but in accordance with those principles which were in use in the times of Jesus.[2]

Did these stories come from an oral source or from a written source? Matt. i. 20–21 gives a little piece of poetry. This is not complete in itself. It was taken from a longer poem. Its contents show that the longer poem contained a fuller account of the story of the annunciation to Joseph. We may therefore say that the story of the annunciation to Joseph and the birth of Jesus was taken from this poem and given by the author of our Matthew in prose with the exception of this extract. This piece has the parallelisms and measures of Hebrew poetry. We may therefore conclude that there was a poem in

---

[1] *Messianic Prophecy,* pp. 63 *seq.*
[2] *General Introduction,* pp. 436 *seq.*

the Hebrew language, which has been translated for the present Gospel.   The other stories do not contain such poetic extracts, and therefore we cannot use the same argument for a written source.   But they are Hebraistic in style.   It is possible that these also were in the same poem; but we have no evidence of it, in their composition or their context.   They may therefore have come from an oral source.   The use that is made of them in the canonical Matthew, to show that Jesus was the Messiah of Prophecy, we may safely say, was not in the source, whether oral or written, but was due to the author of the Gospel himself.

The fullest report of the story of the Infancy of Jesus is given in Luke.   This story is composed of a number of pieces of poetry.   The prose narrative gathers about these ; and is chiefly of the nature of seams to build the poetry together into a harmonious story.   These poems are: (1) The Annunciation to Zacharias,[1] a trimeter poem in the original Hebrew in two strophes of different lengths evidently incomplete in the translation. (2) The Annunciation to Mary,[2] four pieces of trimeter poetry of different

---

[1] Luke i. 13–17.   [2] Luke i. 28, 30–33, 35–37, 38.

lengths connected by seams, evidently incomplete in their present form. (3) The Annunciation to the Shepherds,[1] two pieces of trimeter poetry evidently extracts from a larger piece. (4) The Song of Elizabeth,[2] and (5) the Song of of the Virgin, the *Magnificat* of the Church,[3] both trimeter poems, more complete than the others, but probably also incomplete. (6) The Song of Zacharias, the *Benedictus* of the Church.[4] This seems to be of the pentameter movement. It is uncertain whether we should divide it into five or into two strophes. It is the most complete of the poems, but it is by no means certain that the whole of it has been preserved. (7) The Song of Simeon[5] is a trimeter poem, which is certainly incomplete in the parts of two strophes that have been preserved. This is the *Nunc Dimittis* of the Church.

These seven pieces of poetry are a series of annunciations and of songs of gratitude and praise, all with marked characteristics of Hebrew poetry, not only in form but in the style and substance of the thought. They are not complete in themselves, but extracts from poems.

---

[1] Luke ii. 10–12, 14.

[2] Luke i. 42–45.

[3] Luke i. 46–55.

[4] Luke i. 68–79.

[5] Luke ii. 29–32, 34–35.

This raises the question whether they were not originally parts of larger poems, rather than each from different and independent poems. Six of them have the same trimeter movement, and may be all from the same poem. One of them is a pentameter, like the pentameter preserved in Matthew,[1] and therefore both of these may be from the same poem. May we, therefore, think of two long poems, each giving a poetic account of the birth and infancy of Jesus? Or are we to think of a number of little poems each taking up a different theme? It seems more probable that we have to think of two original poems of this kind, the one chiefly used by Matthew, the other chiefly used by Luke. At all events, so far as Luke is concerned, his story of the Infancy is nothing more than a prose setting for these seven poetic pieces given by him. These poems were certainly originally in Hebrew ; they were also certainly before him in written documents, one or more. They were written sources as truly as the original Mark, and the original Matthew,—all alike in the Hebrew language. They must have been composed before the destruction of Jerusalem, either in the Christian congrega-

---

[1] Matt. i. 20–21.

tion of Jerusalem, or the Christian community in Galilee; therefore by early Christian poets who had access to the family of Jesus, certainly to His brother James the head of the Jerusalem Church, and possibly also to the Virgin Mother of our Lord; and to others who could speak as eye-witnesses or ear-witnesses of these matters embodied in verse. Making every allowance for the poetic form, style, and conception, these poems are sources of the highest value, and of the first degree of historic importance, as belonging with the original Hebrew Gospels of Mark, Matthew, and John, rather than with the later Gospels of Matthew, Luke, and John, as we now have them.

They give us information as to the Infancy of Jesus, and as to the Virgin Mother, which is necessary to complete the story of their lives and to give us a complete understanding of their character. Indeed this gospel of the Infancy as enshrined not only in the first and third Gospels, but also in the Canticles of the Church derived from them, has had more influence upon Christian worship, and no less influence upon Christian doctrine, than the more dogmatic statements of the Epistles. There is no sound reason to reject it as merely legendary, in its material. There is every reason to accept it as giving a valid and essentially historic account of the Infancy of our Lord, so far as it could be reasonably expected in poetic forms.

XIV

OUTLINE OF THE LIFE OF JESUS

THE solution given of the several problems considered in the previous chapters enables us to arrange the material given in
the four Gospels respecting the life of Jesus in
the following outline.

I. *The birth and early life of Jesus.*

The Gospels of Mark and John agree in giving only incidental references to the early life of
Jesus. Mark simply tells us that Jesus was a
carpenter, the Son of Mary, and that He had
brothers and sisters. He was of the royal line
of David and heir to the Messianic promise.[1]
John tells us that He was a Son of Joseph, having mother and brethren.[2] These Gospels defi-
nitely set forth the divinity of Christ and have
no interest in His human development. In this
they agree with the Epistles of St. Paul, which
represent that Jesus was born of a woman, of

---

[1] Mark iii. 31, vi. 3, x. 47.
[2] John i. 45, ii. 1–12, vi. 42, vii. 3–10, xix. 25–27.

the seed of David and Abraham, an Israelite according to the flesh, in the likeness of sinful flesh ; under the Jewish Law, and that He had brothers.[1]   But St. Paul clearly teaches the pre-existence of Christ, and that His entrance into the world was from a pre-existent and divine state.[2]

Almost all that we know of the early life of Jesus is derived from Matthew and Luke. According to these Gospels, the angel Gabriel appeared to the Virgin Mary betrothed to Joseph of the royal line of David, and announced that she had been chosen of God to conceive and bear the Messiah, and that He was to be named Jesus.   Mary was overshadowed by a theophanic cloud and conceived Jesus by the energy of the divine Spirit.[3]   Joseph, instructed by an angel, marries Mary after her conception of Jesus and brings up Jesus as his son and heir.[4]   Jesus was born in Bethlehem, the birth-place of David, a year or two before the death of Herod the Great.   Joseph went up with his wife to Bethlehem, from their home in Nazareth,

---

[1] Gal. i. 19, iii. 16, iv. 4, 5; 1 Cor. ix. 5; Rom. i. 3, viii. 1–4, ix. 5; 2 Tim. ii. 8.

[2] *The Incarnation of the Lord,* pp. 83 *seq.*

[3] Luke i. 26–38.   [4] Matt. i. 18–25.

because it was necessary that he should be regis-
tered in his ancestral home according to the de-
cree of Augustus. The city being overcrowded
he was compelled to lodge in a stable; so that
when Jesus was born, He was cradled in a
manger. His birth was accompanied by a
theophany to the shepherds of Bethlehem, an-
nouncing the birth of the Messiah, and leading
them to the cradle of the infant Jesus.[1] Jesus
was circumcised and named on the eighth day
after birth, and was presented to God in the
temple as the first-born son on the fortieth day
after birth, with sacrifices which imply the
limited resources of His parents at the time.
The presentation was accompanied with a recognition of His Messiahship by Simeon and Anna.[2]
Wise men from the East were guided by a
theophany in the form of a star to Bethlehem,
whither they came to worship Jesus as the new-
born Messianic king. The jealousy of Herod
the king was excited, and, warned by God,
Joseph and Mary escaped from the blood-bath
of Bethlehem, in which Herod hoped he had
slain the infant Jesus in the midst of the
others. They fled to Egypt, where they re-

---

[1] Luke ii. 1–20.　　　　　[2] Luke ii. 21–38.

mained until the death of Herod. Then they returned to Palestine; but not to Bethlehem, for fear of Archelaus, Herod's son; but to their former home in Nazareth.[1] And now a veil is drawn over the life of Jesus, until He was twelve years of age when, in accordance with the Law, He made His first Passover in Jerusalem. He had grown in strength, wisdom and grace. And He was so intent upon learning from the wise men of Jerusalem that He was left behind by His parents when they started on their return to Nazareth. When they missed Him they returned to Jerusalem and found Him in the temple with the rabbis, hearing them and asking them questions. His words to His parents on that occasion make it evident that He was conscious that He was the Son of God in a special sense and that He was called to do His Father's business.[2] But He was also conscious that His time had not yet come, and so He returned with His parents and remained subject to them until He had reached full maturity.[3] Indeed He did not begin His ministry until He was about thirty years of age. Thus, about

---

[1] Matt. ii. 22-23.

[2] *The Incarnation of the Lord,* pp. 42-44.

[3] Luke ii. 40-52.

eighteen years He remained in obscurity in
Nazareth, conscious all the time of His divine
mission, and yet waiting patiently for the time
when He should begin it. During this period
He was, as the carpenter's son, Himself a carpenter, engaged in daily labor with His hands.[1]
In this respect, however, He was doing what the
most distinguished rabbis of the time had done ;
for it was an established principle that each
should learn some trade or handiwork, and the
highest studies were not incompatible with daily
labor.   So St. Paul was a tent-maker, although
certainly trained to the highest degree in the
learning of his times.   There can be no doubt
that the boy who, at twelve, appeared in the
temple, so inquiring, so self-contained, and so
assured of His mission, spent these eighteen
years in the study of the Holy Scriptures and in
all other learning that was accessible to Him.
His wisdom as manifested in His sentences is
more precious in form as well as in substance,
than all the wisdom of Israel.   His skill in
argument as shown in all His discussions with
the Pharisees ; His wonderful parables excelling
all the Haggadistic teaching of the greatest rab-

---

[1] Matt. xiii. 55 ; Mark vi. 3.

bis of Israel, make it evident that Jesus had made Himself master of all that the rabbis of His time had to teach Him and that He easily surpassed them all.

During this period Joseph had probably died. He was evidently somewhat advanced in life when he married Mary. He had at that time children, sons and daughters, from an earlier marriage. There is no good reason to doubt the earliest traditions that Mary retained her perpetual virginity, that Jesus was her only Son, and that Joseph respected her as the consecrated Mother of the Messiah.

II. *Introductory Ministry.*

Jesus began His ministry when He was about thirty years of age.[1] He was prepared for it by His forerunner, John the Baptist, who was a near relative of Jesus on the mother's side, a priest by descent, consecrated from birth to be a prophet like Jeremiah and Ezekiel before him. He preached in the valley of the Jordan, partly in Judæa and partly in Peræa, declaring that the kingdom of God was at hand, that the advent of God and the Messiah was near. He

---

[1] Luke iii. 23

called to repentance and sealed the repentance
with the anointing of Baptism.[1]

Jesus, probably after His return from the
feast of Tabernacles, goes to the Baptist to receive Baptism. The theophany of the heavenly
Voice and the Dove convinced the Baptist that
Jesus was the Messiah : and gave Jesus Himself
the consecration to His ministry.[2] Under the
power of the divine Spirit, and in the ecstatic
state, He remained forty days in the wilderness
of Judæa, absorbed in prayer and meditation.
At the close of this time He undergoes temptations, all directed to the one point of forcing the
issue by a premature assertion of His Messiahship in accordance with the expectations of His
times. Jesus overcomes these temptations and
enters upon His ministry with the same self-
poised, patient and determined purpose that He
manifested eighteen years before. He will be
guided by the divine Spirit upon Him in all His
work. He will not make His mission of none
effect by precipitancy and unwisdom.

Immediately after the temptation Jesus returns to the Jordan, where He is recognized by
the Baptist as the Messiah. Two of the disci-

---

[1] Luke iii. 1–18.   [2] Matt. iii. 13–iv. 11 ; John i. 32–34.

ples of the Baptist, Andrew, and probably John, are transferred to Jesus.[1] On the next day Philip is called to follow Him.[2] With these disciples He goes to Cana of Galilee where He works His first miracle.[3] The disciples return for a short time to their homes, and Jesus doubtless also, to His own home at Nazareth. But in a few days He goes to the shore of the Sea of Galilee and summons the four fishermen to abandon all and follow Him.[4]

A Sabbath of teaching and miracles in Capernaum soon follows.[5]

Jesus retires to a desert place to pray,[6] and then makes His first tour in Galilee preaching in the synagogues and working miracles.[7]

In Capernaum, He heals a paralytic.[8] Soon after He calls Matthew, the publican, to be His disciple.[9] After a farewell supper, at the house of Matthew, Jesus leaves Galilee and rejoins the Baptist in the valley of the Jordan, and the two preach and baptize side by side for a short time. Differences, however, soon emerge between the disciples of Jesus and the disciples of the Bap-

---

[1] John i. 29–42.   [2] John i. 43.   [3] John ii. 1–11.
[4] Mark i. 16–20.   [5] Mark i. 21–34.   [6] Mark i. 35.
[7] Mark i. 35–45.   [8] Mark ii. 1–12.
[9] Mark ii. 13–17 ; Matt. ix. 9–13.

tist, and the Pharisees take advantage of the situation to excite disputes as to purification and fasting and possibly other matters. But the Baptist recognizes that Jesus is his superior. Jesus must increase while he decreases. His preparatory work is wellnigh done. The One for whom he prepared is now at work.[1] Jesus is now more successful in winning disciples than the Baptist.

The attention of the Pharisees is called to Jesus and their jealousy is excited. Accordingly after attending the feast of Passover Jesus prudently returns to Galilee. If we allow two months for the time from Tabernacles to the first departure of Jesus to Galilee after leaving John, we may allow two months for the introductory Galilean ministry, and one month for His work with the Baptist in the valley of the Jordan before Passover.

III. *The Galilean Ministry.*

Jesus now begins in earnest. Thus far He has worked more under the shadow of the Baptist. The centre of the ministry has been where John was baptizing in the Jordan. Very soon

---

[1] John iii. 22–30 ; Mark ii. 18–22.

after Jesus' return to Galilee, the Baptist was arrested and imprisoned, and his work brought suddenly to an end. Jesus therefore becomes the chief, and we may say the only, prophet to whom all eyes were now directed. His ministry in Galilee up to this time had been only preparatory, teaching in the synagogues and working cures. Now He proclaims with more vigor than the Baptist the advent of the kingdom and the call to repentance.

1. The first incident of this second period of Galilean ministry is the plucking of grain from the standing crops, by His disciples immediately after Passover on the sabbath. The Pharisees charge Him with violating the sabbath. The first of the sabbath conflicts begins and the battle with the Pharisees is now on, which is one of the most marked features of Jesus' life. Soon after He teaches the multitudes by the Sea of Galilee, and uses a boat to take Him from place to place.[1] He has, in the meantime, called many other disciples than those six whose calls have been mentioned thus far, and from these He selects a group of Twelve, and gives them a discourse of Consecration which is known as the

-----

[1] Mark iii. 7 *seq.*

Sermon on the Mount.[1] Soon after He heals the centurion's servant.[2] This is only a variation of the nobleman's son.[3] He also raises the widow's son from the dead.[4] These are doubtless only specimens of many miracles and a great abundance of teaching during the fifty days from Passover to Pentecost. At the close of this period messengers came from the Baptist, who, shut up in prison and hearing of the works of Jesus, was somewhat perplexed. He had no doubt of Jesus' Messiahship. But the Messianic ideals of the Old Testament are so complex, the relation of the divine Advent to the several different conceptions of the Messiah is so obscure, that it was quite natural that the Baptist should raise the question whether Jesus was in all respects the one he had heralded, and whether Jesus was not perhaps one of several Messiahs, and another, not yet come, was to fulfil the other ideals.[5] Jesus calls the attention of the Baptist to His works of preaching and His miracles, evidently pointing him to the Messianic prophet of the Second Isaiah.[6] We must

---

[1] Mark iii. 13–19 ; Matt. v.–vii.; Luke vi. 20–49.
[2] Luke vii. 1–10. [3] John iv. 46–54. [4] Luke vii. 11–17.
[5] See *The Incarnation of the Lord*, pp. 167 *seq*.
[6] Luke vii. 18–35 ; Matt xi. 2–19.

probably put at the close of this period the sabbath healing of the man with a withered hand,[1]
which provoked the ire of the Pharisees so that
they conspired with the Herodians to destroy Him.

Jesus now goes to the feast of Pentecost,
and while in Jerusalem heals the infirm man on
the sabbath, and the battle with the Pharisees
begins in Jerusalem.[2]

2. From the feast of Pentecost Jesus returns
for His third Galilean ministry. He partakes of
the hospitality of a Pharisee and accepts the
loving homage of a Magdalene whom He ab-
solves from all her sins.[3] This is probably Mary
Magdalene, who, with other women, accompany
Him and minister to Him on His third tour of
Galilee, mentioned by Luke at the beginning of
his narrative,[4] but by Mark at its close.[5]

This period embraces the four months from
Pentecost to Tabernacles. The incidents mentioned besides these above are : the discourse
representing that His disciples were His real
brethren, rather than His kindred ;[6] the giving
of the parables of the kingdom at the seaside ;[7]

---

[1] Mark iii. 1–6.
[2] John v.
[3] Luke vii. 36–50.
[4] Luke viii. 1–3.
[5] Mark vi. 6 ; Matt. ix. 35.
[6] Mark iii. 31–35.
[7] Mark iv. 1–34.

the crossing the Sea of Galilee and stilling of the tempest ;[1] the visit to Decapolis and healing of the Gerasene demoniac ;[2] the raising from the dead of Jairus' daughter, and the healing of the woman with an issue.[3] These are again only a few of many incidents in a ministry of four months. For the events actually mentioned would have taken only a few days.

Near the close of this period, Jesus learns that the Baptist has been put to death, and that Herod is alarmed for fear that He is John the Baptist risen from the dead. This makes it extremely perilous for Jesus to continue His public ministry in Galilee. Accordingly, having trained the Twelve sufficiently, He sends them forth in pairs in a mission throughout Galilee to carry on His work.[4] It is altogether probable, however, that Jesus always kept one of these pairs with Him, changing them, however, from time to time.

IV. *Ministry in Judæa and Peræa.*

During the absence of the Twelve Jesus goes away from Galilee to carry on His ministry in Judæa and in Peræa.

---

[1] Mark iv. 35–41.   [2] Mark v. 1–20.   [3] Mark v. 21–43.
[4] Mark vi. 7–13 ; Matt. ix. 36 *seq.;* Luke ix. 1–6.

1. He journeys through Samaria to Jerusalem secretly in order to avoid arrest from Herod,[1] and arrives late at the feast of Tabernacles. James and John are with Him on this journey and doubtless remain with Him during all His ministry in Jerusalem. At this feast of Tabernacles, Jesus wrought no miracle, but taught in the temple and had some discussions with the Pharisees.[2] The Sanhedrim sent officers to arrest Him but they were unable to do it.[3] It is probable that it was at this time that the interview of Jesus with Nicodemus took place.[4] At all events Nicodemus at this time defends Him before the Sanhedrim.[5] At this visit to Jerusalem He also visited Martha and Mary.[6] Jesus evidently avoided bringing on a crisis at this feast, for he had determined upon a ministry in Peræa which now begins immediately after Tabernacles.

2. Prior to the going to Peræa Himself, He selects and commissions seventy disciples to go before Him on a mission thither just as He had sent the Twelve on a mission in Galilee. The Gospels give us a number of sayings of Jesus

---

[1] Luke ix. 51–56; John vii. 2–10.   [2] John vii. 11–43.

[3] John vii. 44–49.   [4] John iii. 1–15.

[5] John vii. 50–52.   [6] Luke x. 38–42.

with reference to the special call to disciples, attached to the incident of the scribe who desired to follow Him.[1] Doubtless Matthew is correct in putting them during the previous Galilean ministry. They are given here by Luke as introductory to the Mission of the Seventy.

It is probable that Jesus left James and John behind Him in Jerusalem to continue His mission there; for they were well acquainted there even with the family of the high-priest.[2] It is also probable that Matthew and Thomas joined Him for the Peræan ministry.[3] The first Peræan ministry was for about two months, from Tabernacles to Dedication. The incidents mentioned by Luke as belonging to this period are few. The question of the lawyer as to the way of life, with the parable of the good Samaritan probably belongs here.[4] Jesus teaches His disciples the Lord's prayer.[5] He casts out the dumb demon.[6] He breakfasts with a Pharisee.[7] This is followed by a discussion with the Pharisees. Jesus rebukes a man for coveting a share in the estate of his brother.[8] He warns to

---

[1] Luke ix. 57–62; Matt. viii. 19–22.

[2] John xviii. 15.

[3] See pp. 76 *seq*.   [4] Luke x. 25–37.

[5] Luke xi. 1 *seq*.

[6] Luke xi. 14–29; cf. Matt. xii. 22 *seq*.

[7] Luke xi. 37 *seq*.

[8] Luke xii. 13–15.

repent with reference to the slaying of the Galileans by Pilate and the fall of the tower in Siloam.[1] He heals a woman with an infirmity in the synagogue on the sabbath, and again has to meet the opposition of the Pharisees.[2] These events, with the most of the logia and parables attached, probably belong to this period of the Peræan ministry.

3. Jesus now goes up to the feast of Dedication in Jerusalem.[3] Why He went up to this feast, which was not one of obligation, we are not told; unless the warning of the Pharisees against Herod belongs here.[4] In this case it was for prudential reasons. He was now between Scylla and Charybdis, and the crisis could not long be postponed. Fully aware of this, Jesus had no longer any reason for reserve, and at this feast in Jerusalem He speaks fully and strongly of His Messiahship and His pre-existence.

The story of John[5] tells us that the people were about to stone Him for blasphemy, if He had not escaped from their hands. It also seems necessary to bring in here, John viii. 31–x. 21, giv-

---

[1] Luke xiii. 1–9.   [2] Luke xiii. 10–17.

[3] John x. 22–39.   [4] Luke xiii. 31–33.

[5] John x. 22–39.

ing the assertion of His pre-existence before Abraham, the healing of the blind man on the Sabbath, and the claiming his allegiance to Himself as Messiah ; and also the allegory of the Good Shepherd.

His impending death is clearly in His mind, and He does not hesitate to intimate it in His discourses and discussions. From now on He claims the recognition of His Messiahship.

4. Jesus returns for a brief ministry in Peræa. During this period He takes a sabbath meal with a Pharisee and heals a man with the dropsy.[1] He gives a series of logia to His disciples as to their counting the cost of discipleship,[2] and the three parables of receiving the lost in defence of His own associating with publicans and sinners.[3] Then follow parables of the shrewd steward, and Dives and Lazarus, and other logia and parables.[4] Thus the material belonging to this time is, with a single exception, altogether teaching. Doubtless some of this is out of place, given here for topical reasons. But it is also probable that Jesus avoided publicity, and that therefore He would not work

---

[1] Luke xiv. 1 *seq.*   [2] Luke xiv. 25–35.   [3] Luke xv.
[4] Luke xvi.–xvii. 10.

miracles. He gave His teaching quietly and to
a great extent in private. The Seventy were all
this time engaged in their missions.

5. The Peræan ministry is brought to an
abrupt close by the summons to Jerusalem on
the death of Lazarus. Jesus goes, although as
He and His disciples clearly see, at great risks.
He raises Lazarus from the dead. But this only
attracts the greater attention to Him, and the
Sanhedrim determine to put Him to death.[1]
Accordingly He retires to Ephraim on the borders of Samaria.[2]   After a brief sojourn there He
goes northward through Samaria to Galilee,[3] receiving the recognition of the Samaritan woman
and her friends that He was the Messiah.

V. *The crisis in Galilee.*

It is probable that Jesus' assertion of His Messiahship in the synagogue of Nazareth and His
rejection by His early associates were immediately on His arrival in Galilee.[4]   He was probably
now joined by Andrew and Peter, who accompany Him in His rapid and secret journey northward to Phœnicia,[5] and then along the frontier

---

[1] John xi. i–53.   [2] John xi. 54.   [3] John iv. 4–43.
[4] Matt. xiii. 54–58 ; Mark vi. 1–6 ; Luke iv. 16–30.
[5] Mark vii. 24–30.

to Decapolis, at the northeast end of the Sea of Galilee, where He heals a deaf mute.[1]

Here at Bethsaida, probably, according to appointment, the Twelve all join Him. He is resorted to by multitudes, in the wilderness, and when they suffer from hunger He works the miracle of feeding them. After this the disciples cross the stormy sea, and are diverted from their course, so that they land in the plain of Gennesaret, and make their way to Capernaum. Jesus has joined them. He now delivers His last discourse in the Synagogue of Capernaum.[2] This is connected with discussions with the Pharisees as to His giving them a sign of His Messiahship, and also a dispute as to purification.[3]

Jesus and His disciples now go to Bethsaida, where a blind man is healed.[4] Then a rapid journey northward to Cæsarea Philippi is made. Here Peter, as the spokesman of the Twelve, recognizes Jesus as the Messiah.[5] Jesus now tells them that He is the suffering Messiah, and that He is about to die in Jerusalem and rise

---

[1] Mark vii. 31–37.
[2] Mark vi. 30 *seq.*, viii. 1 *seq.* ; John vi.
[3] Mark vii. 1–23, viii. 11. *seq.* ; John vi. 59.
[4] Mark viii. 22–26.
[5] Mark viii. 27–30, *Messiah of the Gospels*, p. 93.

from the dead.[1]   This is speedily followed by the
Christophany of the Transfiguration to confirm
the faith of the chief apostles.[2]   In the meantime
the other disciples try in vain to heal the demoniac boy ; then Jesus, coming down from the
mount, rebukes them for their lack of faith, and
heals him.[3]

Jesus now rapidly returns to Capernaum on
His way to the last Passover, which was near.[4]
Probably here the incident of the finding of a
shekel in a fish occurred.[5]   The disciples, in
view of the impending establishment of the
kingdom, dispute as to their relative rank in it,
and are rebuked by Jesus.[6]

Jesus journeys to Jerusalem by the ordinary route along the borders of Samaria and
Galilee.[7]   On the way He heals the ten lepers.
He then goes on to make a farewell visit to
Peræa.   On this journey the dispute as to divorce
takes place, then the blessing of little children,
and the giving of counsels of perfection to the
rich young man, and He promises reward to the
faithful disciples.[8]   Jesus in Peræa is rejoined by

---

[1] Mark viii. 31, ix. 1, 30–32.   [2] Mark ix. 2–13.
[3] Mark ix. 14–29.   [4] Mark ix. 30–33.   [5] Matt. xvii. 24–27.
[6] Mark ix. 33–59.   [7] Mark x. 1; Luke xvii. 11; Matt. xix. 1–2.
[8] Mark x. 2–31 ; Luke xviii. 15–30 ; Matt. xix. 3 *seq.*

the Seventy. He now gives several additional logia. He also makes another announcement of His impending death and resurrection,[1] and re-bukes the ambition of James and John.[2] He then leaves Peræa for Jericho, where He heals a blind man and visits Zacchæus.[3]

VI. *Passion Week.*

Jesus arrives in Bethany six days before Pass-over, late on Friday, or the evening which began Saturday. He dines at the house of Simon on this day, is anointed by Mary, and is visited by large numbers of His disciples and others. He spends the night at Bethany.[4]

On Sunday, accompanied by throngs of His disciples, the Twelve, the Seventy, the Galile-ans, the Peræans, the believers of Jerusalem, and a great multitude, He enters Jerusalem as the Messiah. He returns at night to Bethany with the Twelve.[5]

On Monday morning, on His way to the temple, He curses the barren fig-tree. He en-ters the temple, and probably owing to an at-

---

[1] Mark x. 32–34.   [2] Mark x. 35–45.
[3] Mark x. 46 *seq.*; Luke xviii. 35 *seq.*
[4] Mark xiv. 3–9 ; John xii. 1–11.
[5] Mark xi. 1–11 ; John xii. 12–19.

tempt to cheat His disciples in the selecting and
purchase of a Paschal lamb, His indignation is
excited against the traders, and He casts them
out of the temple. He returns to Bethany for
the night.[1]

On Tuesday, on His way to the temple, He
passes the withered fig-tree. He enters into the
temple and finds the Pharisees all ready to chal-
lenge His authority. After a sharp contention
with them He retires from the temple to the
Mount of Olives, and gives His great eschatological discourse to His disciples.[2]

On Wednesday the battle with the Pharisees
is continued. According to a plan devised the
previous day, the Herodians and Sadducees unite
with them in their efforts to entrap Jesus. At
last they are silenced, and nothing remains but to
make out a case against Him and have Him put
to death. On this day, two days before the Passover, the Sanhedrim resolve on His death, and
soon after a bargain was made with Judas to betray Him.[3]

On the morning of Thursday the disciples are
instructed to prepare for the Passover.[4] Jesus,

---

[1] Mark xi. 12–19; John ii. 13–22.

[2] Mark xi. 20–xii. 12 ; xiii.

[3] Mark xii. 13 *seq.;* Luke xxii. 1–6.   [4] Mark xiv. 12–16.

for the last time, visits the temple, meets with some Greeks, hears the theophanic voice, and is finally rejected by the people. He departs from the temple and hides Himself.[1]   At night-fall, the beginning of Friday, Jesus has a farewell supper with the Twelve, after which He institutes the Lord's Supper, and gives the Twelve instruction in a long discourse.[2]   After supper, later in the night, He goes with the Eleven to Geth-semane for His final wrestle and prayer.   Here He is arrested by the officers of the Sanhedrim, Judas betraying Him with a kiss.   He is before morning tried by the Sanhedrim, and, on His affirming His Messiahship under oath, is con-demned to death for blasphemy.   When day arrives, He is sent to Pilate, with a petition for His death, and from Pilate to Herod, and back again to Pilate, who seeks to avoid the responsi-bility for the death of an innocent man.   But Pilate finally yields to the persistence of the Sanhedrim, and, after scourging Him, sends Him in charge of Roman soldiers to be crucified as King of the Jews.   He died at the time of the sacrifice of the paschal victims in the temple, as the great and final Paschal Lamb.   He was

---

[1] John xii. 20 *seq.*   [2] Mark xiv. 17–25 ; John xiii. *seq.*

taken down in haste from the cross, and buried before the Sabbath began.[1]

Saturday was the great sabbath, the first day of the feast of unleavened bread, during which Jesus remained in the grave.[2]

VII. *The Resurrection.*

On Sunday, the day of the Omer offering, Jesus rose from the dead in the early morning. He appeared first to Mary Magdalene and other women,[3] then to Peter,[4] then to Cleopas and another disciple in the afternoon,[5] then to the Ten in the upper room of the Last Supper, Thomas being absent.[6] These four appearances on the day of resurrection were followed by six others. The first of these was on the next Sunday in Jerusalem to the Eleven, Thomas being present.[7] The remaining appearances may all be arranged on successive Sundays, and probably they so occurred, giving thereby to Sunday the name of the Lord's Day, and establishing the custom of

---

[1] Mark xiv. 26 *seq.;* Matt. xxvi. 30 *seq.;* Luke xxii. 39 *seq.;* John xviii. 1 *seq.*

[2] Matt. xxvii. 62 ; John xix. 31.

[3] Mark xvi. 1 *seq.;* John xx. 1 *seq.*

[4] Luke xxiv. 34 ; 1 Cor. xv. 4, 5.   [5] Luke xxiv. 13–35.

[6] John xx. 19–25.   [7] John xx. 25–29.

assembling to meet the Lord on that day. Four of these occurred doubtless in Galilee : on the third Sunday, the appearance to the Eleven on a mountain,[1] on the fourth Sunday, the appearance to the Seven by the Sea,[2] on the fifth Sunday, the appearance to the five hundred brethren at once, and on the sixth Sunday, the appearance to James the Lord's brother.[3]

The disciples then seem to have gone to Jerusalem, where, on the seventh Sunday, the Sunday before Pentecost, Jesus made His final appearance on the Mount of Olives, gave them their final Commission, made His farewell prayer, and ascended to His heavenly throne to reign over the Church and the world as the Messiah, the Son of the Father, the second person of the Holy Trinity.[4]

---

[1] Matt. xxviii. 16, 17.   [2] John xxi. 1–24.

[3] 1 Cor. xv. 6, 7.

[4] Mark xvi. 19 ; Luke xxiv. 50, 51 ; Acts i. 6–11.

INDEX OF SUBJECTS

The Incarnation of the Lord.

8vo.   *Net*, $1.50.

" Such a book, from a man of Dr. Briggs's scholarly standing, in full sympathy with critical conclusions and advanced thought in Scripture interpretation, is exceedingly timely and will be read with great profit and enlightenment by any to whom the divinity of Jesus Christ or the reality of His Incarnation have become in any degree questionable teachings." — *The Advance.*

" We rejoice to believe that the circulation of this book will do great good, and that it will be to many minds a stimulus and a guide in the study of that which is the central fact and doctrine of our Christian faith—the Incarnation of our Lord and Saviour."—*The Churchman.*

A General Introduction to the Study of Holy Scripture.

The Principles, Methods, History, and Results of its Several Departments, and of the Whole.   Crown 8vo. $3.00 net.

Dr. Briggs's new book covers the whole ground of Biblical Study, gives a history of every department, with ample illustrations from the New Testament as well as from the Old, and states the results thus far attained, the present problems, and the aims for the future.   It is written so that any intelligent person can read it with enjoyment and profit.   The work takes the place of the author's *Biblical Study*, which has been extraordinarily successful, and which has been here revised, enlarged to double its former size, and entirely reset, so that it is essentially a new book.

Messianic Prophecy.

The Prediction of the fulfilment of Redemption through the
Messiah. A critical study of the Messianic passages of the Old
Testament in the order of their development. By CHARLES A.
BRIGGS, D.D., Edward Robinson Professor of Biblical Theology
in the Union Theological Seminary, New York. One volume,
crown octavo, $2.50.

"Messianic Prophecy is a subject of no common interest, and this book is no ordinary book. It is, on the contrary, a work of the very first order, the ripe product of
years of study upon the highest themes. It is exegesis in master-hand, about its
noblest business. . . . . It has been worth while to commend this book at some
length to the attention of Bible students, because both the subject and the treatment
entitle it to rank among the very foremost works of the generation in the department
of Exegetical Theology. Union Seminary is to be congratulated that it is one of her
Professors who, in a noble line of succession has produced it. The American Church
is to be congratulated that the author is an American, and Presbyterians that he is a
Presbyterian. A Church that can yield such books has large possibilities."—*New
York Evangelist.*

"It is second in importance to no theological work which has appeared in this
country during the present century."—*The Critic.*

"His arduous labor has been well expended, for he has finally produced a book
which will give great pleasure to Christians of all denominations. . . . . The profound learning displayed in the book commends it to the purchase of all clergymen
who wish for the most critical and exact exposition of a difficult theme ; while its
earnestness and eloquence will win for it a place in the library of every devout lay-
man."—*N. Y. Journal of Commerce.*

"It is rich with the fruits of years of zealous and unwearied study, and of an ample
learning. In it we have the first English work on Messianic Prophecy which stands
on the level of modern Biblical studies, It is one of the most important and valuable
contributions of American scholarships to those studies. It is always more than in-
structive : it is spiritually helpful. We commend the work not only to ministers, but
to intelligent laymen."—*The Independent.*

"On the pervading and multiform character of this promise, see a recent, as well
as valuable authority, in the volume of Dr. Briggs, of the New York Theological
Seminary, on 'Messianic Prophecy.'"—W. E. GLADSTONE.

"Prof. Briggs' Messianic Prophecy is a most excellent book, in which I greatly
rejoice."—Prof. FRANZ DELITZSCH.

"All scholars will join in recognizing its singular usefulness as a text-book. It has
been much wanted."—Rev. CANON CHEYNE.

"It is a book that will be consulted and prized by the learned, and that will add to
the author's deservedly high reputation for scholarship. Evidences of the ability,
learning and patient research of the author are apparent from the beginning to the
end of the volume, while the style is remarkably fine."—*Phila. Presbyterian.*

"His new book on Messianic Phrophecy is a worthy companion to his indispens-
able text-book on Biblical study . . . . What is most of all required to insure the
future of Old Testament studies in this country is that those who teach should satisfy
their students of their historic connection with the religion and theology of the past.
Prof. Briggs has the consciousness of such a connection in a very full degree, and
yet he combines this with a frank and unreserved adhesion to the principles of modern
criticisms. . . . . He has produced the first English text-book on the subject of
Messianic Prophecy which a modern teacher can use."—*The London Academy.*

The Messiah of the Gospels.

By CHARLES A. BRIGGS, D.D., Edward Robinson Professor of Biblical Theology in the Union Theological Seminary, New York. Crown 8vo, $2.00.

The Messiah of the Apostles.

By CHARLES A. BRIGGS, D.D., Edward Robinson Professor of Biblical Theology in the Union Theological Seminary, New York. Crown 8vo, $3.00.

Prof. BRIGGS in these two volumes takes up the ideas presented in the author's "Messianic Prophecy of the Old Testament," and traces their development in New Testament prophecy. The method and scope of the work are entirely original, and it is full of fresh statements of the doctrine of the person and work of Christ as the result of the new point of view that is taken.

"It is learned, sound, evangelical, and is a useful contribution to the Christological literature of the day."—*New York Tribune.*

"It requires but a cursory examination of this book to discover that it is the work of a profound Biblical scholar. It will prove a valuable aid to the Biblical student, and is well worthy of a place in his library."—*Reformed Church Messenger.*

"The book, as to far the larger part of it, is one of the best and most precious ever written upon the person, the offices, the work of the Son of God and Son of man. The author has the Scriptures thoroughly at command, and without quotation-marks repeats the very words, adding passage to passage, phrase to phrase, with splendid and overwhelming power."—*The Christian Intelligencer.*

"Like all Dr. Briggs' books, the work though given in lucid and ringing English has depth and breadth of learning."—*Boston Zion's Herald.*

"As we lay the book down we have a renewed sense of the courage, independence and erudition of the author."—*The Churchman.*

"He has given to us on the whole a noble contribution of devout scholarship towards an understanding of the Christ of New Testament teaching."—*Richmond Religious Herald.*

" . . . . it is a book of great merit, and one that no student of the New Testament can afford not to read with candor and diligence."—*The Examiner.*

"The whole tone of the discussion is adapted to impress one with the idea that the writer is a sincere lover of and seeker after truth. The whole volume will be found very helpful to any diligent student of the Scriptures."—*Pittsburgh Presbyterian Messenger.*

"The work, by its freedom from contentiousness and by its respect for other learned opinion, claims a dignified place in contributions to historical theology."—*The American Historical Review.*

"Dr. Briggs is to be congratulated on having brought to a successful termination this truly remarkable series of volumes on one of the most important themes of Biblical study. The Christology of the New Testament is likely to wait long for a more competent and more successful expositor."—*The Christian Register.*

"Whoever makes a faithful study of this book will put himself under the guidance of an admirable teacher, and will come into close contact with the living Word of the divine revelation."—*The Congregationalist.*

The Bible, the Church, and the Reason.

The Three Great Fountains of Divine Authority. By CHARLES A. BRIGGS, D.D., Edward Robinson Professor of Biblical Theology in Union Theological Seminary, New York. Crown 8vo, $1.75.

" It consists of lectures delivered at different times since the recent assault upon him. In these lectures he does not indicate the least inclination to beat a retreat, cry for quarter, or even secure a truce. And yet, with some few exceptions, he does not exhibit personal feeling, nor defend himself personally from the charges made against him. He simply elaborates and substantiates the positions in his inaugural which have subjected him to public criticism and to a possible trial for heresy."—*The Christian Union.*

" The problems which are discussed with masterly power in this volume are not those of Presbyterianism, or of Protestantism, but of Christianity, and, indeed, of all Biblical religion. To any man for whom the question of God and revelation has an endlessly fascinating interest, the book will prove suggestive and stimulating. We cannot see why even the Israelite and the Roman Catholic should not desire to taste—despite the traditions of synagogue and Mother Church— this latest forbidden fruit of the tree of knowledge."—*The Literary World.*

The Higher Criticism of the Hexateuch.

By Prof. CHARLES A. BRIGGS, D.D., of Union Theological Seminary, New York. New Revised and Enlarged Edition. Crown 8vo, $2.50.

SUMMARY OF CONTENTS: The Testimony of Scripture—The Traditional Theories —The Rise of Criticism—The Documentary and Supplementary Hypothesis— Date of Deuteronomy—Development of the Codes—Witness of the History—The Argument from Biblical Theology and its Results—Recent Discussions.

It is with the aim of contributing to a better understanding and higher appreciation of the documents of the Bible that the book has been written, which is designed for the general public rather than for Hebrew students, and, for the most part, technical material been put into the Appendix, which constitutes a considerable part of the volume. This new edition is the result of a thorough revision of the entire work, and contains numerous additions of importance. It is also characterized by a thorough study of the types of Hebrew law and the history of Hebrew legislation. It should therefore be of great interest to the legal profession.

"The volume before us gives in plain language Dr. Briggs's belief. No minister can afford to be ignorant of the subject, or of Dr. Briggs's position."—*The Christian Enquirer.*

Whither?

A Theological Question for the Times. By CHARLES AUGUSTUS BRIGGS, D.D., Edward Robinson Professor of Biblical Theology in the Union Theological Seminary, New York. Third Edition. One volume, crown 8vo, $1.75.

"He shows that genuine Christianity has nothing to lose, but much to gain, by unfettered thought and by the ripest modern scholarship ; that the doctrines which progressive theology threatens are no essential part of the historic faith, but rather outworn garments, woven with warp and woof of tradition and speculation ; that being hung upon the noble form of Christianity, have obscured its real proportions, and that 'the higher criticism' of which timid and unscholarly souls are so much afraid, is really making the Bible more manifestly the book of God, by relieving it from the false interpretations of men."—*The Press*, Philadelphia.

"The book is a strong one. It is packed with weighty matter. Its reach is larger than any of the author's other works, though its compass is smaller. It contains only 300 pages, yet it is a critical treatise on Westminster and modern theology, and also on church life and Christian unity. It is written in nervous, virile English that holds attention. It has unusual grasp and force. The title and the chapter headings suggest compression : 'Whither?' 'Drifting,' 'Orthodoxy,' 'Changes,' 'Shifting,' 'Excesses,' 'Failures,' 'Departures,' 'Perplexities,' 'Barriers,' 'Thither.' There is a whole history in some of these words, and a whole sermon in others."—*The Critic*, New York.

"At the same time it is irenic both in tone and tendency. It is noble from beginning to end, though the author may possibly place unnecessary emphasis on the organic unity of the different denominations of Christendom as the condition precedent for a true catholic unity. There is not a touch or smell of rationalism or rationalistic speculation in the book, and freely as the author deals with his opponents, it is an honest freedom, which will promote good feeling even amid debate."—*The Independent.*

American Presbyterianism :

Its Origin and Early History, together with an Appendix of Letters and Documents, many of which have recently been discovered. By CHARLES A. BRIGGS, D.D., Edward Robinson Professor of Biblical Theology in the Union Theological Seminary, New York. 1 volume, crown 8vo, with Maps. $3.00.

"The Presbyterian Church owes a debt of gratitude to the enthusiasm and antiquarian research of Professor Briggs. He seems to have seized the foremost place among them, and his vigorous, skilful, and comprehensive researches put all Protestant Christians, and especially Congregationalists, under obligation to him."—*Boston Congregationalist.*

"This is an admirable and exhaustive work, full of vigorous thinking, clear and careful statement, incisive and judicious criticism, minute yet comprehensive research. It is such a book as only a man with a gift for historical inquiry and an enthusiasm for the history and principles of his Church could have produced. It represents an amazing amount of labor. Dr. Briggs seems to have searched every available source, British and American, for printed or written documents bearing on his subjects, and he has met with wonderful success. He has made many important discoveries, illustrative of the Puritan men and period, useful to himself, but certain also to be helpful to all future inquiries in this field."—*British Quarterly Review.*

CHARLES SCRIBNER'S SONS, Publishers,

153-157 Fifth Avenue, New York.